A Cyclist's Spirituality:

Spiritual Lessons Learned from Riding a Bike

FR. JOHN BULLOCK, LC

Dedication

To Mom for having driven me to my bike races when I was a teen, as well as having always supported me in my priestly vocation.

To The Blessed Mother for her maternal care in my life.

Table of Contents

FR. JOHN BULLOCK, LC

A Cyclist's Spirituality:

Spiritual Lessons Learned from Riding a Bike

FR. JOHN BULLOCK, LC

INTRODUCTION

Why does our spiritual journey require such effort?

"Do you not know that the runners in the stadium all run in the race, but only one wins the prize? Run so as to win. Every athlete exercises discipline in every way. They do it to win a perishable crown, but we an imperishable one."

1 Corinthians 9:24-25

St. Paul predated this booklet's connection between sports and the spiritual life by about two millennia. He notes that our spiritual journey, like a foot race, entails a goal, effort, and the need for discipline. I believe the comparisons are innumerably more.

The question may arise in the minds of many as to why the spiritual life requires so much effort. Would that not be an attempt at "earning" salvation, which is ultimately a gift from God?[1] Doesn't St. Therese of Lisieux teach us that we should simply allow God to carry us up in his arms to his Kingdom?[2] The Catechism of the Catholic Church states that while faith is a gift, it may be lost. As such, we must fight to retain that grace and to grow in it.[3] Therefore, to correspond to the gift of grace and faith we must "Run so as to win."

This is where a cyclist's spirituality enters the equation.

What is a cyclist's spirituality?
Why this booklet?

When I was 14 years old, I caught the road-cycling bug. At first, I simply wanted to tour with a bike. It quickly became a passion for racing. By the time I was 16, I road close to 50 miles a day, was a United States Cycling Federation (USCF) Category 4 rider[a] , occasionally raced, and planned on becoming a professional. I wanted to be in the Tour de France. I had a goal, was disciplined, and was riding to win.

Bad knees put that dream to rest about two years after it had begun. I was heartbroken at the time, but life continued. Not long after graduating from college, I entered the seminary of the Legionaries of Christ. I am happy as a Catholic priest. Cycling, so I thought, was simply a long-lost love. Then about 10 years ago, I casually tried riding again to see what would happen. To my surprise, I was able to ride much more than I thought possible. Therefore, after an almost 30-year interval, I once again ride enough to consider myself a cyclist. I am neither fast nor do I race, but the passion is still there.

a   USCF is the abbreviation for United States Cycling Federation. Category 4 is the entry level for riders. The USCF was integrated along with several other racing disciplines into USA Cycling.

In my return to riding, I have discovered that cycling has had a real impact on my spiritual life. There are several things that cycling teaches me about the spiritual life, and inversely, there are things in my spiritual life that I bring with me on my rides. I am constantly seeing parallels between my two loves.

This booklet is a collection of short reflections on spiritual lessons that we can learn from cycling, as well as a few ways in which we can bring our faith to cycling. This mutually enriching relationship between the sport and faith is what I dub "a cyclist's spirituality." At the end of each reflection, there will be a Scripture passage and some questions to ponder. At the end of the book there is a list of suggested readings.

CHAPTER 1

Bike Type and Fit

The kind of bike we get depends upon the type of riding we plan to do: road bike, mountain bike, cycle-cross, gravel, crossover, or track. My hunch is that most cyclists focus primarily, if not exclusively, on one type of riding. Even among road bikes there are a variety of options: touring, racing, or aero. The specificity continues with other factors such as the frame's material, stiffness, and the like.

Once a cyclist chooses a bike, he or she should get a professional bike fit. If someone rides a significant amount, the correct frame size and saddle height matter – a lot. In his autobiography The Climb, four-time Tour de France winner Chris Froome recalls how simply having his saddle one centimeter too high caused both saddle sores and an inflamed knee.[4] Even as a casual rider, I have found it quite helpful to install a horizontally shorter headset to avoid leaning too far forward while riding. A bicycle's specs matter a great deal.

Once the proper fit is made, no two bikes will be exactly alike since our bodies are unique – some with longer torsos in relation to their legs, others the opposite, and so on.

This specificity of each person applies to the spiritual life as well.

While we all start with the same "bike" – our common human nature with a body and soul – each person is unique. Referring to the Church, St. Paul writes,

> "For as in one body we have many parts, and all the parts do not have the same function, so we, though many, are one body in Christ and individually parts of one another. Since we have gifts that differ according to the grace given to us, let us exercise them" (Romans 12:4-6).

The different types of bicycles – road, mountain, etc. – are like the different vocations in life. In the Catholic Church, we recognize that most people are called to marriage, some to the priesthood, others to religious life (like St. Teresa of Calcutta), and some to the single life. Each person has the same goal of serving both God and neighbor but goes about it according to the context of his or her particular vocation. The unmarried layman might have more time to dedicate to his or her career as a means of service to others. The mother of several small children has still another well-defined mission. The priest serves by teaching, accompanying, and bringing the sacraments to his community.

Our Unique Vocation

Similar to a bike fit, those sharing the same vocation will do so in a variety of ways. In my own congregation, the Legionaries of Christ, while we have the same spirituality and mission, each person approaches it from a different angle. Some are academics, others are in governance, some are spiritual guides, and still others are well-known public speakers.

While we all belong to various communities – a family, a parish, a company, etc. – we are never reducible to any one community or category. Every human person is unrepeatable. Even identical twins are clearly distinguishable from each other with their distinct personalities and outlooks on life.

When asked about how many paths there are to salvation, Pope Benedict XVI responded, "just as many… as there are people."[5] He was implying that God has a unique relationship with each person – a particular "fit." There are a great variety of ways to pray, to encounter God, and to respond to him. In the Gospels, Jesus frequently adapts his manner to the person with whom he is speaking. He is theological with Nicodemus. He speaks of sowing and harvesting to farmers. He speaks of politics to Pilate.[6] God not only respects our uniqueness; he is the one who made us so.

However, just as a personalized bike fit does not negate the fundamental principles of cycling, so too this personalized relationship with God does not negate certain universal principles about God and man. For example, there are rules that we must follow if we want to thrive, such as eating well, or, on a moral level, being honest. We are human beings who share a common humanity, and yet each one of us is unique.

Like seeking out professional help to get a good bike fit, so too we should take care to get help in discerning our own particular vocation within the Church. We should seek the advice of someone who understands well the principles of the Christian life: a priest, a religious, or even a well-formed layperson. If our particular vocation has long since been decided, it still does not hurt to have some occasional feedback, since we may need some minor adjustments to help us stay the course.

For Further Reflection

"Jesus saw Nathanael coming toward him and said of him, 'Here is a true Israelite. There is no duplicity in him.' Nathanael said to him, 'How do you know me?' Jesus answered and said to him, 'Before Philip called you, I saw you under the fig tree'."

John 2:47-48

Some Questions

1. In what ways is my relationship with Jesus unique?

2. How did I discern my vocation in life?

3. How do I experience his presence and action in my life?

4. At this point in my journey, are there any shifts needed in the living of my vocation – a new phase, an adjustment, a renewal?

CHAPTER 2

Join the Club

I most frequently ride alone. I can keep my own pace, pray, and gather my thoughts. However, even I, somewhat of a cycling hermit, enjoy the occasional ride with others. Whether a person races, tours, or just rides casually, somewhere along the line he or she will most likely ride with someone else, whether that be simply riding with a friend, or joining USA Cycling, a race team, a riding group, or a gran fondo .[a]

Professional racing is exciting to watch because it is a team sport. There is a great deal of strategy occurring within the dynamics of the peloton[b] , the breakaway[c], the sprints, and so forth – with each team working to get its captain to win. Is your man in the breakaway ? Is your main opponent in it? Do those in the peloton reel it in or let it go? Who will do the work? If your team does, will you have enough energy at the end to win? If you do not push, will you miss your opportunity?

When we follow the sport of cycling as fans, we rarely do so as individuals. We must share and debate about our favored

---

a   Gran fondo – a usually large and publicly organized group ride.

b   Peloton – the main group of riders during a race.

c   Breakaway – The smaller group of riders that goes off the front during a race.

riders in any given race – the more passionately disputed, the more fun.

Aside from racing, riding in a group means trying to keep up or waiting for the others. Personally, I prefer to keep up with stronger riders if I can, but I have learned to also enjoy the relaxed journey with others on a casual ride. The former makes me a better rider while the latter reminds me that cycling is meant to be fun and not just about time goals. Either way I benefit from at least occasionally riding with others.

Even when riding alone along a trail I frequent, there remains among the more committed riders a certain comradery. We recognize the "real" riders quickly enough: they have the kit, the bike, and sufficient velocity. We recognize the mutual passion and commitment to the sport that money alone cannot purchase. When passing each other going opposite directions there is the "insider's " nod that means we are part of the group. (I must confess that I really appreciate receiving the nod.) Other times, while riding in the same direction, we notice someone going about the same pace and the two of us decide to ride together for a bit (and even converse some).

Now with the internet and programs such as Zwift, even indoor training at home can be done connected to others – either on the same virtual ride, or simply by posting times and comparing them.

All this is to say that cyclists form a type of community around a common passion with its own culture, rules, and expressions.

We form community in all that we do because we are social beings created for community. As Cardinal Ratzinger put it:

"[The] inclination to love, to form a relationship with someone else, is inbuilt in [man]. He is not an autarchic, self-sufficient being who develops alone, in isolation, not an island unto himself, but essentially created for relationship. Without relationship, in an unrelated state, he would destroy himself. And it is precisely this basic structure of his being that reflects God. For this is a God whose essential being, in just the same way, rests on relationships, as we learn from the doctrine of the Trinity."[7]

The Community of the Church

The Church is also a community. The Catechism states, "In the Church, God is 'calling together' his people from all the ends of the earth."[8] There are beginners, casual members, and those who are more fully dedicated. There are different vocations, dioceses, parishes, and movements. But there is the common family united around Jesus Christ, his Church, his teaching, and the sacraments.

When we decide to follow Jesus, it is within the community of the Church. Again, Ratzinger says,

"I cannot just make Christ my private possession and try to keep him for myself. To a certain extent, the discomfort of belonging to his family goes along with Christ himself. Faith has been bestowed on us in this community context; it is not otherwise available."[9]

The Church also has a certain culture, behavior, and even lingo that outsiders will not easily understand. It takes effort to be a part of the whole.

We believe by faith that the community of the Catholic Church, unlike other human communities, was founded by Jesus and is being guided by the Holy Spirit. It is this presence and guidance that gives us the confidence to ride in tandem with the Church and in so doing that we may reach the finish line safely.

Nevertheless, as with any community, within the Church we must learn to get along, individually and collectively – to speed up to keep up, or to slow down to wait up. It is both a challenge and a benefit. Learning to live with others and to follow the captain makes us less selfish and more open to others, and ultimately more open to God.

For Further Reflection

"When they entered the city they went to the upper room where they were staying, Peter and John and James and Andrew, Philip and Thomas, Bartholomew and Matthew, James son of Alphaeus, Simon the Zealot, and Judas son of James. All these devoted themselves with one accord to prayer, together with some women, and Mary the mother of Jesus, and his brothers."

Acts 1:13-14

Some Questions

1. Do I believe in Jesus' presence in the Catholic Church?

2. Do I believe the Catholic Church is guided by the Holy Spirit?

3. Am I willing to learn from others, adapt to others, and serve them?

4. How do I build community?

5. What is most difficult about community life? What do I most enjoy?

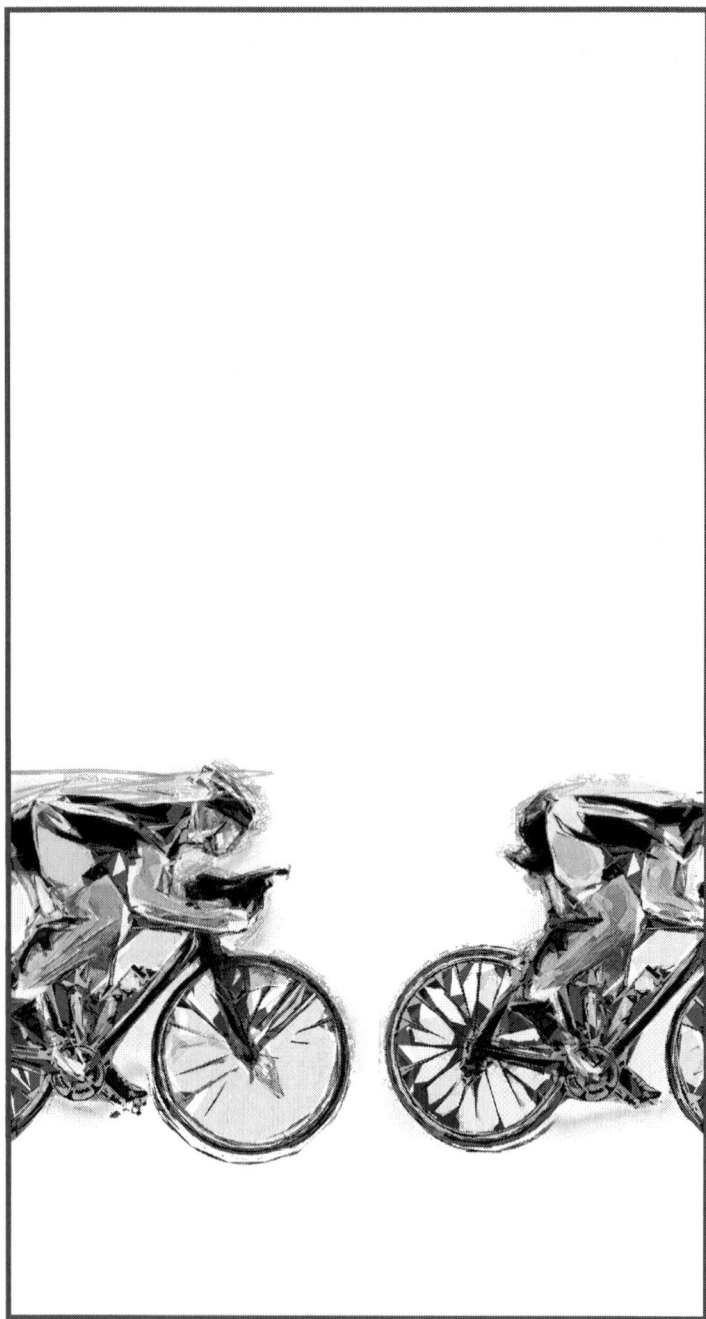

CHAPTER 3

Drafting

Drafting in cycling is when one rider follows closely behind another to take advantage of the slipstream created by the rider out front who is blocking the wind.[10]   When drafting off someone, we can save about 30% to 40% of our energy.[11]

Except for individual time trials, drafting is perhaps the single most decisive factor in racing. The more people who take turns "pulling" at the front, the more dispersed the effort is, and the more energy saved per rider. That is why an individual or a small group breakaway rarely succeeds if the peloton is determined to catch them. The peloton simply has more people who can take a turn pulling at the front than does the small group and can therefore sustain faster speeds for longer. Nevertheless, if the breakaway is sufficiently large enough and working well together, and the peloton is somewhat complacent or waits too long to respond, then the breakaway has a chance of success.

Each team will protect its captain or sprinter by having him or her pull as little as possible during much of the ride, to save energy for crunch-time. On the flip side, if they can isolate another team's leader from his or her team, that leader will have less chance of success. If the crosswinds are strong, this makes positioning and drafting all the more urgent because the difference in energy expenditure between pulling and drafting will be even greater. If a rider loses the lead group or echelon, it is important to form a new echelon quickly rather than battle the wind alone.[12]

Watching the pros ride in a team-time trial of eight or so people is amazing. The time-trial bikes, aero-gear, and matching outfit are fascinating, but the real clencher is seeing the riders work together like a well-oiled machine following each other so closely. Depending on the conditions and distance of the course, pro team time trials can average up to 35 miles per hour.[13]

Drafting helps the recreational rider go faster and farther. Ideally, equally strong riders share the load evenly. In practice, this is rarely the case. On any given day, some riders are stronger than others. The stronger rider has to decide whether to do more than his or her fair share of pulling. Equally, if the group is seeking speed, the weaker rider has to be willing to be pulled rather than slowing the group by trying to pull too much. For this to work well, the stronger rider will have to exercise self-sacrificing charity, while the weaker rider will have to have the humility to accept it.

To be honest, when I am in a group ride, I am usually one of the weaker ones – and that is hard to accept. However, when due to pride I insist on pulling faster and farther than I should, then I hit a wall pretty quickly and force the group to really slow down and wait for me. Instead, I should accept the kindness offered me.

Christians Helping One Another

In our life as Christians, we all have moments when we should "pull" for our neighbor, and at other times allow ourselves to be pulled. None of us are so strong that we will never need help, or so weak that we cannot help others in some way.

How can we help? The Church gives us the broad categories of the corporal and spiritual works of mercy – that is, to help the body and the soul respectively.

> "Instructing, advising, consoling, comforting are spiritual works of mercy, as are forgiving and bearing wrongs patiently. The corporal works of mercy consist especially in feeding the hungry, sheltering the homeless, clothing the naked, visiting the sick and imprisoned, and burying the dead. Among all these, giving alms to the poor is one of the chief witnesses."[14]

Reaching out to our neighbors in need lets them know we care. Christian charity is perhaps our most authentic means of drawing others closer to God. It has been said, "Preach always, and use words when necessary."

True charity requires self-sacrifice. Pulling is hard work. We may spend time with someone who is lonely. We may teach someone a new skill. We might speak out against an injustice. Our work may create employment opportunities for others. These and numerous other possibilities will require us to let go of something for the sake of the other. Therein lies the beauty. In a concrete way, we are saying, "Right now, you are more important to me than I am to myself." That is love. As

Jesus said at the Last Supper, "No one has greater love than this, to lay down one's life for one's friends." [15]

Equally important is to receive the kindness of others. We should be open to accepting help when others offer it, or when they offer us constructive criticism. It is equally important to accept the gifts and gratitude that others offer us. It is OK to not always be OK. We are not always fine. We may need to seek out a priest for confession or advice. We may need a counselor. We may need help finding a job or paying a bill. We may simply need a friend to listen.

Let others pull us when we are weak. Once restored to the group and strengthened, we may return to pulling others.

For Further Reflection

"Then the king will say to those on his right, 'Come, you who are blessed by my Father. Inherit the kingdom prepared for you from the foundation of the world. For I was hungry and you gave me food, I was thirsty and you gave me drink, a stranger and you welcomed me, naked and you clothed me, ill and you cared for me, in prison and you visited me.' Then the righteous will answer him and say, 'Lord, when did we see you hungry and feed you, or thirsty and give you drink? When did we see you a stranger and welcome you, or naked and clothe you? When did we see you ill or in prison, and visit you?' And the king will say to them in reply, 'Amen, I say to you, whatever you did for one of these least brothers of mine, you did for me.'"

Matthew 25:34-40

Some Questions

1. How do I most frequently assist others?

2. What are my gifts and opportunities to serve?

3. Where do I find it difficult to reach out to help others?

4. Am I willing to accept the kindness of others?

CHAPTER 4

The Pain & the Prize

We have all been there. Perhaps it was a race, a gran fondo, a long tour, or simply a long ride aiming for a certain time limit. We trained for it weeks in advance. We ate well the evening before. The morning of, we packed all the essentials – from a spare inner tube to energy drinks and gels – and we set off. We started off well, keeping pace with our competitors, fellow riders, or time goals, and for the most part we were enjoying the ride. And then it happened, possibly gradually, or more often than not, all of a sudden. Our energy drained, the lactic acid began building up in our calves and thighs, our neck and shoulders grew stiff, and we began to slow down. Perhaps we hadn't yet officially "bonked," but we were approaching it quickly.

Then the dreaded question came: "Why am I doing this again?"

Cycling is a rewarding experience – even exhilarating. Still, cycling at any serious level is not easy, and definitely not comfortable. In those moments when it hurts, which will come, it becomes very important to keep the immediate goal in mind. Make it to the finish line!

However, if we want the finish line to motivate us, we have to renew our conviction that we can actually finish. There are some practical things we can do. First, we can set intermediate goals: "Just make it to the crest of this hill," only to aim for the next hill afterwards. Secondly, instead of thinking, "I have 14 miles to go," we can think, "I have less than 15 miles to go." "Less" is a powerful word when we are in pain. We first have to conquer mind and heart before we conquer the hill.

The enjoyment of a really tough ride is primarily after the fact: We did it! We conquered the route, we set a personal best, or at least finished well." The joy didn't come despite the difficulty, but through it. Conquest only comes through battle. And yes, we can enjoy even the pain-filled battle while battling. We want to push ourselves to the limit. We want to see what we can achieve. We want to leave it all on the field – or on the route. Non-cyclists suspect we cyclists enjoy suffering just a bit too much.

Finishing the Race as a Christian

There is a reason St. Paul compared Christianity to an athlete training for a race (cf. 1 Corinthians 9:24-25).

Following Christ is a rewarding experience – even exhilarating. Still, when we take our spiritual and vocational commitments seriously, we can feel the pinch and ask ourselves, "Why am I doing this again?" To be fair, Jesus warned us that following him would not be easy: "Whoever wishes to come after me must deny himself, take up his cross, and follow me" (Matthew 16:24).

Here too, we must keep our eyes on the prize – the ultimate one being heaven - rooted in the conviction that we can really make it there. That is the point of the theological virtue of hope. It is "theological" because this hope is a gift from God to help me get to God – just as are faith and charity.[16] Specifically, hope helps us to "desire the kingdom of heaven... as our happiness, placing our trust in Christ's promises and relying not on our own strength [to get us there, but because]... 'he who promised is faithful.'"[17]

Belief in God's fidelity is always a surer foundation than belief in our own strength, but the two are not meant to be in competition. When we are convinced that God has our back, it empowers us to dig deep and give our all precisely because he is with us.

Similar to cycling, attention to intermediate goals helps us along the way. They show us that we are going in the right direction and strengthen our conviction that we can make it to the end. So, we recognize and celebrate spiritual and vocational landmarks throughout our journey - marriage, ordination, or religious profession; the birth of that first child or that first assignment as a priest or nun; advancement in one's career or a success in ministry, etc. Put succinctly, the long-term goal is to be with God and love him in heaven, whereas the short-term goal is to love God now by loving our neighbor, primarily through the faithful fulfillment of our duties.

Therefore, prepare well for the ride, expect the struggle, and hope in his grace to get us there.

For Further Reflection:

"And another said, 'I will follow you, Lord, but first let me say farewell to my family at home.' [To him] Jesus said, 'No one who sets a hand to the plow and looks to what was left behind is fit for the kingdom of God.'"

Luke 9:61-62

Some Questions:

1. Am I aware that my life is a journey with a concrete destination?

2. Do I focus on the finish line of heaven? Do I place the means to get there such as Mass, Confession, and prayer?

3. Do I find myself frequently getting frustrated along the way?

4. How do I respond to such frustrations?

CHAPTER 5

Travel Light

II was 15 years old, and still aspiring to be a professional cyclist, when I also got my first real job as a paperboy. Save the Sunday edition, which needed delivering by car and thus Mom's help, I would deliver the weekday editions in the afternoon by bike. The bike alone, my mom's old bike, probably weighed about 35 pounds. The saddlebags for the papers and the wooden frame that sustained them probably weighed 20 pounds. Then there were the papers weighing still another 15 pounds or so. Not surprisingly, it was really hard to pedal. I was so slow that it was easy for the ankle-biting breed of Yorkshire Terrier to, well, actually bite my ankle! (He had had his shots.)

My first "racing" bike was an old, beat-up, 10-speed Schwinn that probably weighed close to 30 pounds. When I got my first real road bike, a Raleigh, about a year later, it was at least 7 to 10 pounds lighter. I noticed the difference immediately.

Professional cyclists and their teams will go to amazing lengths to lighten their bikes by even a fraction of a kilo, since a slightly lighter bike can make a real difference, especially in a stage race where the overall standings are largely decided in mountain stages.[18] For the sake of competitive fairness, the UCI, or

International Cyclists' Union[a], prohibits a bike to weigh less than 6.8 kg or 14.99 pounds.[19]

Those who tour with their bike and carry all their own gear would also want to keep their weight to a minimum. Five to 10 pounds less luggage probably goes a long way in making the ride more doable and enjoyable.

The moral of the story: Travel light.

Shedding Spiritual Baggage

The less excess baggage we carry in the spiritual life, the better. Traditionally, that baggage is referred to as "attachments." In other words, we may be attached to certain people, places, things, or plans that keep us from putting God and his will in the first spot. "No one can serve two masters. He will either hate one and love the other, or be devoted to one and despise the other. You cannot serve God and mammon" (Matthew 6:24). Our Lord's point is not against us having possessions; the Church has frequently defended the right to private property.[20] However, we should not let things become our "master."

Something becomes our master, or idol, when it replaces God's primacy in our hearts. Everything else becomes subservient to the "most important thing in my life." Chasing after money could cause all other values like friendship, family, health, and even God to fall by the wayside. The same could be said

---

a The UCI or "Union Cycliste Internationale" (International Cycling Union) is the main governing body of professional cycling

of alcohol, power, fame, comfort – pretty much any creature. Idolatry is to treat a creature as God, the only one who merits absolute allegiance, because only he is absolute.

Now, created things are not bad in and of themselves. God created them for our good. Even money, a human invention, is not inherently evil. Where we must take care is how we relate to things. Things are meant to be means to an end, or tools to achieve the good, our ultimate good being union with God. If money helps us fulfill our responsibility to provide for our family, assist the needy, create job opportunities for others, and pursue other good endeavors, then it is helping us serve God and others.

Even human relationships should help and not hinder our relationship with God. Our spouse, our family, and our friends are meant to bring us closer to God. That can occur through a joyfully enriching relationship or, at times, through a difficult one that may draw us closer to God in our need. But relationships that lead us to sin need changing or, at times, dropping altogether. We have all had relationships which have pulled us away from God, such as that "drinking buddy"- with whom we may have frequently gotten drunk.

A disordered attachment or an idol that goes unchecked has the tendency of becoming a tyrant. Think of Scrooge in Dicken's A Christmas Carol who only thought about money but had no family or friends. Think about the alcoholic or drug addict that is destroying his or her life because he or she cannot break the habit. Think of the man addicted to pornography who is enfeebling his ability to love his wife as well as to treat women with respect.

Religious (monks and nuns) take vows of poverty, chastity, and obedience to be signposts for the importance of detachment in the spiritual life. Their lifestyle does not declare that money, marital love, and independence are bad, rather that they should be subordinate to God. Their vows shout "God is enough for me," so that those called to marriage, to own private property, and to a degree of independence remember that even they must put God first.

Therefore, as we order each possession and relationship in our lives to God, they will not take on more weight than they should. Our journey to God will be a lighter one.

OK, now for the tough question: Can our bike and biking become an idol?

As a religious priest I have often asked myself that question. I love cycling. Do I love it too much? Ultimately, for the religious and the layperson, the question remains the same: Does cycling bring me closer to God and to the fulfillment of my vocation, or hinder it? That is something each person has to prayerfully answer. Potential warning signs include: Would I skip Mass to go for a bike ride? Do I spend more time riding, working on the bike, and following the sport than I do in prayer and spending time with my family? If so, recalibrate. Put first things first. Take time for prayer and family responsibilities, and then, if those things are in order – enjoy the ride.

For Further Reflection:

"As for you, do not seek what you are to eat and what you are to drink, and do not worry anymore. All the nations of the world seek for these things, and your Father knows that you need them. Instead, seek his Kingdom, and these other things will be given you besides."

Luke 12:29-31

Some Questions:

1. Are there things, projects, attitudes, or people that I place above God? What do I need to do to correct the unbalance?

2. What does it look like to relate to people, work, and projects so that they may help me and others draw closer to God and each other?

3. When did I last have a strong experience of encountering something or someone that strengthened my relationship with God?

4. How can cycling improve my relationship with God? (Hint: That's the topic of this entire book.)

CHAPTER 6

Fuel for the Journey

When still riding as a teenager, I did not think too much about the importance of proper nutrition in relation to riding. I just liked eating. As such, on the return trip of my usual bike route, I would stop by a French bakery to pick up a croissant. Wow, it would almost melt in my mouth! My love for France is not limited to the Tour.

Popular wisdom considers two things in the relationship between food and cycling. The first is that it is ill-advised to ride soon after a large meal. The second is that if people ride a lot, then they can basically eat whatever they want and as much as they want – since cycling burns so many calories. There is some truth to both statements.

Nevertheless, professional cyclists and dedicated amateurs realize that eating and cycling have a much more nuanced relationship. For the body to respond well to riding, especially longer or more intense rides, the when, what, and how of eating matters. Cyclists have to store up energy before the ride, top it off during the ride, and help the body recover after the ride.[21] Before a longer ride, they should have a rich carbohydrate dinner and a slow-release carbohydrate breakfast, like oatmeal.[22] During the ride they should drink water (a bottle for each hour), adding electrolytes to at least one bottle. It's also important to eat during the ride to sustain energy levels and keep from "bonking." Eating smaller quantities of energy bars, fruit, or gels throughout a ride is most helpful. After the ride, an energy drink and rice can help recover the carbohydrates and proteins lost during the ride. Finally, the truly dedicated would want to keep an eye on their overall diet for both cycling and general fitness.[23]

Therefore, we need fuel for the journey. What we eat matters, since to some degree we are what we eat.

Spiritual Nourishment

The same can be said about our spiritual journey. We need the proper fuel, or we burn out. Three ways to feed our souls are contact with Scripture, prayer, and reception of the Eucharist.

Firstly, we need to strengthen and nourish our spirit by coming in contact with the Word of God in Sacred Scripture. The Second Vatican Council of the Catholic Church in its document on the Word of God states,

> "The sacred synod also earnestly and especially urges all the Christian faithful, especially Religious, to learn by frequent reading of the divine Scriptures the 'excellent knowledge of Jesus Christ' (Philippians 3:8). 'For ignorance of the Scriptures is ignorance of Christ.'"[24]

Catholics systematically hear most of the Bible in the Sunday Mass (the readings – Old and New Testament – have a three-year cycle). However, we should also read, study, and meditate on Scripture outside of Mass. Scripture is, if you will, spiritually healthy nourishment.

Secondly, we need to pray daily if we want to deepen our relationship with God. Any relationship requires time and dedication. In that sense, our relationship with God is no different. A daily prayer routine should have different moments spread throughout the day in which we lift heart and mind to God – the very definition of prayer.[25]

- One way of praying is "mental prayer." We usually start with Scripture or a good spiritual book, reading a brief passage, and then prayerfully reflecting on what we just read. This reflection should lead to connecting with God with or without words. Our aim in prayer – to connect with God – is what distinguishes this from study. We should take care to spend more time conversing with God than we do reading the material. I recommend that people meditate in the morning for at least 10 minutes daily.

- For Catholics, another good way to lift heart and soul to God is through the rosary. The goal is to contemplate (imagine and reflect) on the mysteries of Christ, whereas the words of the vocal prayers (the Our Fathers and Hail Marys) are like the background music to the movie of the life of Jesus. If an entire rosary seems too daunting, get in the habit of praying one mystery (or "decade") a day – this takes five minutes. (Later in this book, I'll share my experience of praying the rosary on the bike).

- A third way to pray is to do a "conscience exam" daily, preferably toward the end of the day – but not waiting to the point when we are already falling asleep. We should reflect on the graces God has given us that day, thank him for them, and then consider how we have responded. If we did well, we should thank him for that. If we did poorly, we should tell him we are sorry, and that with his help we will try to do better. It's good to finish with a simple resolution for the next day. This too need not take much more than five minutes.

Finally, and most importantly, Jesus left us his Body and Blood in the Eucharist as food for our journey. The Church holds that the Eucharist is not merely a symbol, but actually "the Body and Blood, together with the soul and divinity, of our Lord Jesus Christ and, therefore, the whole Christ is truly, really, and substantially contained."[26] Chapter 6 in the Gospel according to John contains an entire Eucharistic discourse; its central message is "I am the living bread that came down from heaven; whoever eats this bread will live forever; and the bread that I will give is my flesh for the life of the world."[27] When we receive the Eucharist worthily at Mass, Jesus draws us closer to himself and we receive the spiritual strength needed to keep going. However, to fruitfully receive the Eucharist and truly benefit from it, we must approach it with faith and a conscience clear of any grave sin.[28] (More on confession later).

Just as professional cyclists grab their "musette," or lunch bag, on the go to fuel up for the rest of the ride, we Catholics must take time for Scripture, prayer, and the Eucharist. As a result, we'll ride better, longer, and happier on our way to the finish line.

For Further Reflection:

"'I am the living bread that came down from heaven; whoever eats this bread will live forever; and the bread that I will give is my flesh for the life of the world.' The Jews quarreled among themselves, saying, 'How can this man give us [his] flesh to eat?' Jesus said to them, 'Amen, amen, I say to you, unless you eat the flesh of the Son of Man and drink his blood, you do not have life within you. Whoever eats my flesh and drinks my blood has eternal life, and I will raise him on the last day. For my flesh is true food, and my blood is true drink. Whoever eats my flesh and drinks my blood remains in me and I in him. Just as the living Father sent me and I have life because of the Father, so also the one who feeds on me will have life because of me. This is the bread that came down from heaven. Unlike your ancestors who ate and still died, whoever eats this bread will live forever.'"

John 6:51-58

Some Questions:

1. Do I have a daily routine of reading Scripture and doing mental prayer? Do I pray the rosary?

2. Am I consistent with my daily prayer routine? What hinders it or helps me to stick to it?

3. Do I have a living faith in the Real Presence in the Eucharist?

CHAPTER 7

Training

When I first started racing at age 14, I knew little to nothing about cycling. However, what was clear was that if I wanted to start winning races, I needed to train – a lot. So, train I did. When I was 16, my daily training sessions would consist in 50-mile rides. And it showed. For my age, I was a strong rider and could even race against adults, although I must admit that in the Houston area in the early 1980s, racing was a pretty underdeveloped sport and the racing community consisted of very few people.

I did not know what I was doing. I had no trainer or coach. And it showed. After probably pushing too hard a gear for too long, combined with an apparent propensity to arthritis, my knees basically "gave out" at age 16, and stopped me from pursuing my cycling career.

We must train intensely and intelligently.

Professional teams have been fine-tuning the training process for generations. It is amazing to see the level of precision professionals will attain in their training and in their overall approach to gain a competitive edge.

To train for the Tour de France, teams must prepare the entire year with a combined training and racing schedule for each rider to "peak" (be at their best performance level) during the Tour – or whatever race they set as their annual priority. When the training season begins, around January, the riders must build their aerobic base and spend 20 to 31 hours on the bike each week, but at a lower intensity.[29] After two months of the initial stage, riders transition to higher-intensity workouts to build fitness.[30] Then, once they are racing (earlier in the season and before the Tour) or training at a higher level, they must allow for more recovery time in correlation with the intensity.[31]

Professionals also pay great attention to detail in the various facets of racing to improve their competitive edge. Worth particular mention is David Brailsford's philosophy of marginal gains as applied to cycling. As head of Team Ineos, formerly Team Sky, Brailsford has sought to improve the efficiency of his riders by minimally improving countless aspects by just 1%, such as diet, aerodynamics, winding down after the race, improving the sleep of the riders, etc. This has led the team to winning seven of the last ten Tours de France.[32] In other words, enough small changes make a big difference.

Training for Holiness

To follow Jesus means to live like him. That is a very tall order – if you will, the moral equivalent of riding in the Tour. To even begin to do so, we need the help of his grace, but it also requires our effort. A long-standing saying in the Church is that grace elevates nature, not replaces it. So, in addition to receiving his help through the sacraments and prayer, we must train ourselves to live virtuously, or to form good habits.

Here, too, we must work intensely and intelligently.

Keenly aware of our many faults, where do we begin? To simplify focus and increase our efficacy, we do not concentrate so much on the outward expressions of our sinfulness, but rather we look at the root causes or attitudes that lead to such expressions. We call such inclinations or attitudes which lead to sin as "root sins." There are three root sins: pride, vanity, and sensuality.[33]

> "When speaking of 'root sins,' however, spiritual writers are looking at the deep-seated tendencies toward selfishness that we have inherited because of original sin. These are tendencies to seek our happiness outside of communion with God. They are not vices per se, because they didn't come about as the result of repeated personal sins. Rather, they make up the raw material from which vices spring. We can correct vices by forming virtues, but we can never completely eradicate ('de-root') our tendencies to selfishness. They always remain to be battled against."[34]

Pride is the attitude of a sense of self-superiority and self-sufficiency in relation to others, even God. We have to have the last word. We know best. We need no help.

Vanity is when we desperately seek the approval of others. Peer pressure becomes the decisive factor for the vain person.

Sensuality is where we seek to satisfy our senses above all else. "Feeling good" becomes the priority whether that be related to emotions, food, or the sexual drive.[35]

Now, a healthy self-respect, consideration for relationships and the feelings of others, emotional satisfaction, food, and the sexual drive are good things in and of themselves. They become problematic when self-affirmation, the approval of others, or simply feeling good are more important than truth, responsibility, charity, and God.

While everyone struggles with all three root sins, most people can identify primarily with one of the three. How can we know if we struggle mostly with pride, vanity, or sensuality? We ask ourselves, "Where do I most commonly fail, and what underlying attitude causes it?" It's the "there I go again" sin we want to identify and gradually correct – by focusing on the root. So, if we are constantly arguing because we believe ourselves always right, we might pick pride as our root sin. If laziness or being overly emotional is an issue, it might be sensuality. If peer pressure controls us, it might be vanity.

Once we have identified the root sin, we pick the contrary virtue to counteract the inclination, a kind of antidote. Then we exercise that virtue daily by frequently repeated small actions.

- Fight pride with humility, which is accepting the truth of our being creatures and sinners, not groveling. We can practice the following: Listen better. Acknowledge the good ideas of others. Speak well of others. Don't have the last word. Show gratitude to other people and to God.

- Fight vanity with purity of intention, which is doing things for the right reasons – love of God, duty, charity. Some concrete exercises in purity of intention include: Perform hidden acts of kindness. Do things joyfully even when not thanked. Spiritually offer up a difficult task to God.

- Fight sensuality with discipline, which puts what is good above what "feels" good. Some concrete exercises in discipline include: Get up as soon as the alarm sounds. Keep a morning routine. Stick to a prayer, exercise, or work routine. Clean up one's room. Be cheerful even when one's feelings don't cooperate.

Again, while everyone has to struggle to a degree with all three root sins, we usually want to stay focused on our primary root sin, which will likely remain a lifelong battle. Can we eventually change it up? Yes, but we must take care to see that sufficient progress has been made on the main culprit before adjusting.

It is important to examine daily how we are doing. Did we do what we set out to do? Did we practice this virtue? Ideally, this is done within the context of prayer. This is not simply reflecting on a self-help program, but rather a prayer that considers our effort at growth with God. This can be part of the daily conscience exam, which may last three to five minutes.

After time, and ideally with a spiritual director (coach) to assist in the process, we should see real progress (but not perfection). Just like cycling, we must work intensely and intelligently. As St. Paul writes, "I do not run aimlessly; I do not fight as if I were shadowboxing. No, I drive my body and train it, for fear that, after having preached to others, I myself should be disqualified" (1 Corinthians 9:26-27).

For Further Reflection:

"Which of you wishing to construct a tower does not first sit down and calculate the cost to see if there is enough for its completion? Otherwise, after laying the foundation and finding himself unable to finish the work the onlookers should laugh at him and say, 'This one began to build but did not have the resources to finish.'"

Luke 14:28-30

Some Questions:

1. Am I practical, concrete, and systematic in my training for cycling? Do I do the same for my spiritual and moral life?

2. What root sin, or disordered inclination, seems to be causing me the most trouble – pride, vanity, or sensuality? What is the contrary virtue I should seek to fortify in response?

3. Can I list four to five concrete – and small – examples of how to exercise daily the desired virtue?

4. Do I have a set time to do a conscience exam, so I can reflect on, among other things, how I did in living my concrete virtue?

CHAPTER 8

Threshold Workouts & Intervals

Whether racing or touring, road cycling requires endurance, but speed matters too. Even if we just tour, it helps to increase our average speed so we can cover more ground in less time. But if we want to become a faster and stronger rider, we must go faster during training. There are basically two approaches to doing this: intervals and threshold work.

Intervals, also known as high-intensity interval training (HIIT), means alternating between brief spurts of maximum speed (sprinting) and moments of recovery. The duration of the sprint may be a few seconds, a minute, or more. The recovery may be of similar duration.[36] So we sprint as fast as we can for one minute and then cool down by easy spinning for another minute, and repeat this pattern several times.

Similarly, threshold work is "the hardest effort you can sustain"[37] for an extended period – such as 20, 30, or 60 minutes.[38] It is like an extended sprint, although obviously not as fast paced as a 60-second effort.

Whether doing intervals or threshold work, pushing ourselves hard - very hard - can bring positive results – no pain, no gain. However, we must take care not to overdo it; otherwise, what was meant to be helpful ends up bringing fewer results or even becoming detrimental. Both approaches must alternate with recovery rides.[39]

Spiritual Intervals

The same holds true in the spiritual life. There will be moments of intense strain – or the cross – and moments of recovery - or consolation.

If we look back on our own lives, we will probably recognize the pattern. There are phases in our family, professional, and spiritual lives where most everything seems like a steep up-hill climb. Work projects fall through, family relationships are strained, and God seems awfully silent during prayer. Questions like "Where are you, God?" and "What am I doing wrong?" often rise to the surface. We can be tempted to throw in the towel in all, or at least many, areas of life. On the flipside, there are moments when everything seems to be going well. The family is united, mutually supportive, and joyful. Work is interesting and profitable. Prayer is interesting, enlightening, and consoling.

Couldn't our spiritual, familial, and work lives be an ever-growing crescendo from good to better? The answer is ultimately "yes," but "better" does not equate to easier – at least not initially. This is where the analogy of cycling is quite apropos. After a series of well-calibrated high-intensity workouts, we should be better cyclists. It just isn't easy to get there. Similarly, to grow in the spiritual life, we must often be tested or pushed to our limit to grow. Jordan Peterson writes that:

> "winning at everything might only mean that you're not doing anything new or difficult. You might be winning but you're not growing, and growing might be the most important form of winning. Should victory in the present always take precedence over trajectory across time?"[40]

How are we supposed to increase in faith if God does not allow us the opportunity to experience moments that test our faith at its current "level"? How are we supposed to grow in patience if we do not have opportunities to exercise it – sometimes rather intensely? If we are to grow in any human or spiritual virtue – which is simply a good habit – we need intense practice.

Good news! We have a perfect trainer in God. Whatever comes our way, because he actively wills it or passively permits it, will never be more than we can handle if we rely on his grace. He will neither allow us to be tempted beyond our capacity to resist evil nor tested beyond our capacity to withstand it.[41]

> "God is faithful, and he will not let you be tempted beyond your strength, but with the temptation will also provide the way of escape, so that you may be able to endure it" (1 Corinthians 10:13).[42]

Let's clarify a couple of points. Firstly, God never actively chooses moral evil; that would be an inherent contradiction of his moral goodness and holiness. He does, however, respecting our freedom as moral agents, permit us to choose evil.[43] Secondly, God himself does not tempt us to sin, but he does permit it, since resisting temptation can help us to better realize where we still need to grow.[44] Finally, we must distinguish "between trials, which are necessary for the growth of the inner man, and temptation, which leads to sin and death." [45]God may choose the former for our good, but only permit the latter.

In other words, if we face all trials and temptations with God and in obedience to his will, we can handle any difficulty – or cross - that comes our way. Additionally, the great effort such a cross entails should help us become better Christians, better persons. For example, many married couples often admit that it was precisely the difficulties in life that drew them closer together. It is a human and spiritual improvement through high-intensity training. This is the context for St. Paul's passage in Romans, "We know that all things work for good for those who love God" (Romans 8:28).

Therefore, we should not be afraid when we struggle, but undertake the difficulty – with God – as high-intensity training for life or, if you will, "cross training."

For Further Reflection:

"Then Jesus said to his disciples, 'Whoever wishes to come after me must deny himself, take up his cross, and follow me. For whoever wishes to save his life will lose it, but whoever loses his life for my sake will find it. What profit would there be for one to gain the whole world and forfeit his life? Or what can one give in exchange for his life? For the Son of Man will come with his angels in his Father's glory, and then he will repay everyone according to his conduct. Amen, I say to you, there are some standing here who will not taste death until they see the Son of Man coming in his kingdom.'"

Matthew 16:24-28

Some Questions:

1. Do I do high-intensity or high-intensity interval training on my bike? Have I seen results in my riding?

2. Have I ever considered moments of difficulty in life as opportunities to train in faith, hope, love, perseverance, and patience?

3. How quickly do I turn to God in prayer during difficult moments?

4. Have I ever reflected on graces received through difficulties in life? Did I recognize God's providential care in those moments?

CHAPTER 9

Avoid Dangerous Roads

I recently moved. As any avid cyclist would do, one of my first tasks upon arrival was to scope out the best and closest bike paths. I was fortunate that a lovely 17-mile paved bike trail through the woods was only about six miles from my new house. Naturally, I decided to ride my bike on the roads to the trail and back. One day, after having made the trip to the trail on my bike several times, I came to a red light at an intersection. Both the road I was on and the intersecting one had two lanes going each direction. While waiting at corner by the curb for the light to change, a pickup truck decided to get around me to turn right on red. He pulled into the intersection just a few feet from me only to notice far too late that another pickup was coming at him at around 50 mph. Collision seemed inevitable, and the truck trying to turn was going to be hit – hard – right into me. Thank God the oncoming driver was able to change lanes to avoid hitting the truck, but not without overcorrecting and grazing the car facing him which was waiting to turn left. Again, thank God no one was hurt, but the police, fire department, and ambulance had to come to the scene. Shortly after, I was convinced to drive my car to the trail and ride only on the trail.

Road cycling requires, well, roads. The problem is that we often have to share those roads with cars. Most drivers are careful and conscientious, but with so much traffic on certain roads, we quickly encounter the 1- or 2% of reckless drivers. In any collision between a car and a cyclist, the cyclist will always lose.

Dangerous drivers seem to have become an increasing problem for professional cyclists, who need to spend large amounts of time training on roads. For instance, Chris Froome got hit by a driver while training. Fortunately, he was not hurt.[46] Less fortunate was Michele Scarponi, who died that same year after colliding with a van during training.[47] The whole Giant-Alpecin Team was hit head-on by a car while on a training ride, which injured six riders, at least two seriously.[48]

Now, it is impossible to avoid all danger. We run risks as soon as we get on our bike. The point is to minimize the risks. I imagine professional teams go through great lengths to find safe areas to train. Amateurs have to rely on their own common sense and possibly the advice of fellow riders to find safer riding routes.

Spiritual Dangers

Similarly, we should also avoid unnecessary moral and spiritual dangers. This has traditionally been referred to as avoiding the occasion of sin, which is simply, "Any person, place, or thing that of its nature or because of human frailty can lead one to do wrong, thereby committing sin."[49] Sin is a decision to do wrong.[50] The occasion are the circumstances – more or less likely (proximate or remote) to lead someone to sin.[51] For example, if going out with a drinking buddy always ends up in our getting drunk, then we would want to avoid going out with him or her.[52] We want to make the effort to avoid scenarios that are more likely to lead us to sin.

Since our inclination to sin is something we carry within our own fallen nature,[53] we cannot perfectly avoid every single remote occasion for sin. To do so could easily become a form of scruples in which we fear that everything is sinful, like being afraid of all roads when we cycle because we might crash. Instead, we must take care to avoid the circumstances which are most likely to lead us to trouble.

Additionally, based on differences in personality and experiences, some things may be an occasion for sin for some while not for others. For one person, hanging out in a bar and having a couple of drinks with friends doesn't lead to temptation toward drunkenness in the least, whereas another person may have such an addiction to drink that even passing a bar in the street is a problem.

We are called to live life joyfully and freely. Usually, the best way to avoid moral problems is to keep our focus and energy on doing good things, so that there is less time and energy for sin or scruples. Nevertheless, an honest assessment of which roads to avoid in order to have a safe and enjoyable ride is an essential part of riding a bike and of following Christ.

For Further Reflection:

"If your hand causes you to sin, cut it off. It is better for you to enter into life maimed than with two hands to go into Gehenna into the unquenchable fire. And if your foot causes you to sin, cut it off. It is better for you to enter into life crippled than with two feet to be thrown into Gehenna. And if your eye causes you to sin, pluck it out. Better for you to enter into the kingdom of God with one eye than with two eyes to be thrown into Gehenna."

Mark 9:43-47

Some Questions:

1. How careful am I in choosing good and safe roads on which to ride? Do I take the same care with spiritual and moral situations?

2. What circumstances or relationships should I avoid?

3. Have I become too fearful or simply seen life as avoiding sin or problems? Or, do I tend to be cavalier and careless in regard to situations that might lead me to sin?

4. What helps me stay positively and joyfully on task regarding the good in my life?

CHAPTER 10

Crashes Happen

Despite our best efforts to choose good roads and riding conditions, crashes will happen.

Once when I was riding on the road of a local park – with cars but at a very low speed limit – I was going downhill at a pretty decent clip. Just then a car which had been parked perpendicular to the road pulled out right in front of me and, upon seeing me approach, stopped. I was now in danger of either going full-speed into the side of the car and flipping over it, or sliding out and going under it as I tried to avoid it. Only a few inches from the car, I was able to swerve around it and remain upright on my bike. It seemed as if the laws of physics were just slightly bent in that moment. I believe in guardian angels.

At other times while riding, I have had relatively minor tumbles in which scrapes and/or bruises resulted – at least twice, I must confess, due to my being distracted by looking at my phone.

A friend of mine hit a pothole on a group trail ride and went over the handlebars, landing headfirst. He had to be airlifted and was in a coma for a short period. Thank God he fully recovered.

Whether an accident results in minor scrapes or a life-threatening incident, the reality is that there are varying degrees of crashes, and if the rider survives, the reaction is the same: recover and learn from the experience. Obviously, recovery can be as simple as getting up, brushing off the dirt, and getting back on the bike, or as complicated as surgery and months-long rehabilitation.

Spiritual Crashing

Similarly, we have moral crashes. We sin.

Sin is not a mistake: "Oops, I accidentally knocked over the lamp." For someone to be personally culpable, he or she must know that the action is morally wrong and still freely choose to sin. If we're honest, we are all aware of having freely chosen to sin, to do wrong.

Just as there are varying degrees of crashes, there are also varying degrees of sin. The more serious ones are referred to as "mortal," whereas the smaller ones are called "venial." What is the difference? For a sin to qualify as "mortal" there has to be grave matter, full knowledge, and full consent.[54] What qualifies as grave matter? The Catechism states,

"Grave matter is specified by the Ten Commandments, corresponding to the answer of Jesus to the rich young man: 'Do not kill, Do not commit adultery, Do not steal, Do not bear false witness, Do not defraud, Honor your father and your mother.' The gravity of sins is more or less great: murder is graver than theft. One must also take into account who is wronged: violence against parents is in itself graver than violence against a stranger."[55]

As to the effects of the sin on the soul, venial or minor sins wound the charity or presence of God's grace in one's soul,[56] whereas mortal sin "destroys charity in the heart of man by a grave violation of God's law; it turns man away from God." [57]

What do we do? We recover and learn from the experience.

The best recovery possible is the sacrament of Confession, where through the person of the priest, Jesus offers forgiveness and grace to the repentant sinner.[58] The Church teaches that: "All mortal sins of which penitents after a diligent self-examination are conscious must be recounted by them in confession."[59] While not necessary to mention venial sins in confession, it is nevertheless a good practice to do so to "form our conscience, fight against evil tendencies, let ourselves be healed by Christ and progress in the life of the Spirit."[60]

While the Church obliges us to confess only once a year,[61] it is very helpful to go more frequently, perhaps once a month, to fortify our relationship with Jesus, to rely more deeply on his grace, and to continue to form our conscience.

Finally, to learn from our crashes, it is also important to continually form our conscience by studying the Church's moral teachings. Donald DeMarco, a Catholic philosopher, aptly wrote,

> [There is a commonly held opinion that] "no authority, other than one's own conscience, has the right to dictate personal moral choices to anyone... This popular and commonly held view of conscience is false even to the meaning of the word 'conscience.' Etymologically, the word 'conscience' (in Latin < con + scientia) literally means 'with knowledge.'

One's conscience cannot be formed in an intellectual void. Conscience, to be properly formed, requires knowledge."[62]

We form our conscience by assimilating the word of God in faith, prayer, and practice; examining our conscience; receiving aid from others and grace; as well as being "guided by the authoritative teaching of the Church."[63]

With the aid of grace that comes from confession, our study of the Church's moral teachings, and our ongoing efforts to live as God wants, we will notice real progress in our spiritual and moral life.

Crashes happen. The important thing is to recover, learn, and grow.

For Further Reflection:

"On the evening of that first day of the week, when the doors were locked, where the disciples were, for fear of the Jews, Jesus came and stood in their midst and said to them, 'Peace be with you.' When he had said this, he showed them his hands and his side. The disciples rejoiced when they saw the Lord. [Jesus] said to them again, 'Peace be with you. As the Father has sent me, so I send you.' And when he had said this, he breathed on them and said to them, 'Receive the Holy Spirit. Whose sins you forgive are forgiven them, and whose sins you retain are retained.'"

John 20: 19-23

Some Questions:

1. How willing am I to admit to my failings and sins? Do I tend to make excuses for and obfuscate my sins?

2. Am I good at apologizing to people and to God?

3. Have I developed the habits of examination of conscience and regular confession?

4. Do I study the moral teachings of the Catholic faith? Do I work hard to understand them?

CHAPTER 11

Jesus Is the Captain Acting as a Domestique

Professional cycling is a team sport. In today's world of professional cycling, it would be rare, almost impossible, for an individual to power to victory solely by his or her own strength. Therefore, in addition to the strength of the individuals that comprise a team, team unity and cohesion are essential for success.

For team cohesion to function well, the role of each individual must be clearly defined. In cycling we have the captain, or leader, for whom the rest of the team, the domestiques (French for "servants")[64], are working to get the win. The domestiques sacrifice their own chance of winning in the process – pulling at the front of the team train, getting water bottles from the team car in the caravan behind the peloton, and even giving the leader their bike if necessary.

Most of the time teams function well under such a system. Working for the common goal of a team victory keeps each rider motivated to do his or her part. Not surprisingly, however, teams have had instances of real division or breakdowns of the members' defined roles. Now at times, teams may approach a race or a stage with, "let's see who has the best legs," and then support that person. At other times it is simply the case of an individual breaking ranks to pursue his own glory at the expense of the team, such as a domestique who of his own accord attacks and leaves the leader behind. There are many famous examples of teams being clearly divided during the grand tours.

However, there was one dramatic example in a relatively recent Tour de France that did just the opposite. The original team leader willingly embraced the role of domestique once he realized that his domestique was better positioned to win the Tour. It was the 2018 Tour de France, and the captain-turned-domestique was the four-time Tour winner Chris Froome of Team Sky. His domestique-turned-captain was Geraint Thomas. Now Thomas had been a faithful domestique to Froome in Froome's previous Tour victories, so there was a relationship of respect, loyalty, and friendship. But it still must have been very hard for someone as competitive as Chris Froome to give up the team leader role. Nevertheless, he did, and as a result, Geraint Thomas won that Tour.[65] From the perspective of the team, they went with the individual best poised to win. From Froome's perspective, there was a dying to self for the good of the team. This story is well told in an article by Ken Turley.[66]

Servant Leadership

We see the logic of the leader turned servant time and again in the person of Jesus Christ – "the Son of Man did not come to be served but to serve" (Matthew 20:28). He fed the hungry, cured the sick, drove out demons, and taught the crowds. He ultimately gave his life for us on the cross. Jesus lived for others, and he insists that his followers do the same.

> "So when he had washed their feet [and] put his garments back on and reclined at table again, he said to them, 'Do you realize what I have done for you? You call me "teacher" and "master," and rightly so, for indeed I am. If I, therefore, the master and teacher, have washed your feet, you ought to wash one another's feet. I have given you a model to follow, so that as I have done for you, you should also do'" (John 13:12-15).

In my own spiritual journey Jesus Christ is clearly the boss. However, I have received so much more from him than he has from me. He truly is a servant leader. In our relationship with God, it is God who takes the initiative, whereas we respond. He created us. He died for us on the cross. He invited us into his family, the Church, through baptism. He has – time and again – forgiven our sins. He has called us to follow him. He has given us a mission, companions, opportunities for growth, consolations, and graces – countless graces – along the way.

Ultimately, the only thing we can offer directly to God is our "yes." We may decide to accept his gifts and his graces and, with his help, we may decide to embrace our vocation, or the mission, which he has given us. But that vocation entails serving Jesus indirectly in the needs of my brothers and sisters. "Amen, I say to you, whatever you did for one of these least brothers of mine, you did for me" (Matthew 25:40).

At times I have visualized myself as drafting off of Jesus, who rides in front of me – the captain pulling his servant. Now, I may respond to Christ's service of "pulling" me along in my ride by "pulling" others in return. The Church is meant to be one long echelon in an amazing team time trial on the road to Heaven.

For Further Reflection:

"Then an argument broke out among them about which of them should be regarded as the greatest. He said to them, 'The kings of the Gentiles lord it over them and those in authority over them are addressed as "Benefactors"; but among you it shall not be so. Rather, let the greatest among you be as the youngest, and the leader as the servant. For who is greater: the one seated at table or the one who serves? Is it not the one seated at table? I am among you as the one who serves.'"

Luke 22:24-27

Some Questions:

1. How aware am I of the countless gifts God has given me, and continues to give me?

2. How good am I at showing gratitude to God and to others? How do I express it?

3. How quick am I to help others? When I hold back, why?

4. How can I best serve God in my family, in my neighbor, in the stranger?

CHAPTER 12

We Have Our Heroes

Very early in my cycling days, around the age of 15, I discovered "Winning Bicycle Racing Illustrated" magazine. It introduced me to the European professional circuit, both past and (then) present.[67] The covers of the magazine, as well as its interior, were filled with glossy images of the greats: Eddy Merckx, Bernard Hinault, Greg LeMond, and Andy Hampsten – to name a few. I would devour every issue I could get into my hands. These were my heroes. They were who I wanted to be – professionals riding in the Tour de France, the Giro, and the Classics!

Any fan of the pro tour would admire and respect most all of the pro riders for the fact that they made it to the pros. Nevertheless, we have our personal favorites among them. More recently I have admired Chris Froome for his ability to climb, his tenacity in the face of difficulty, and his gentlemanly demeanor. On the other hand, I also like Peter Sagan for his explosive power, determination, bike-handling skills, natural showmanship, and his evident ability to still have fun on the bike. I like Primož Roglič for his strength, tenacity, and ability to rebound from disappointment, as well as the cross tattooed on his forearm and the public witness to his faith that it implies. I greatly respect Lizzie Deignan for her combative spirit on the bike and her willingness to put her career on hold, twice, to have a child.

We want to imitate those whom we admire. While riding as a teen, I would do things like hold onto the brake levers and wear my cap backwards, simply because it was what I saw my heroes do. I am not alone. There are countless cycling articles and videos about what the pro riders do: their riding techniques, what they wear, what they eat, how they train, etc. Admiration leads to imitation. We realize that we will most likely not get to their level, but we can improve by learning something from them nevertheless.

Finally, we would love the opportunity to meet some of our cycling heroes one day. Autograph- and selfie-seekers at events are natural expressions of appreciation and enthusiasm on the part of fans.

The Saints

Like cycling, we have our heroes in the Church; they are the saints.

> "The Church's official recognition of sanctity implies that the persons are now in heavenly glory, that they may be publicly invoked everywhere, and that their virtues during life or martyr's death are a witness and example to the Christian faithful."[68]

The saints are our older brothers and sisters in Christ who have been officially recognized as examples for us to live by, and intercessors in Heaven for us to invoke.

We admire all the saints for the mere fact that they are saints. We even honor them as a group on "All Saints Day" on November 1st. Nevertheless, we have our favorites with whom we somehow most identify and "connect." In addition to the Blessed Mother, some of my favorites include: St. Paul, St. Patrick, and St. John Paul the Great – primarily for their passionate love for Christ and their clear missionary zeal.

Here too, admiration should turn to imitation. What can we pick up from the example of the saints? Can we pray a little more like them? Can we live charity a bit more like them? Yes, we imitate Christ, the Son of God and the very source of sanctity, but we also try to imitate the saints, who are reflections of Christ.

Now, if we want to admire and imitate the saints, we must get to know them. We do that primarily by reading the stories of their lives. There are collections of short stories on the saints as well as more thorough biographies. I find those stories most helpful that do not hide the saints' struggles – both interiorly and exteriorly. For example, how consoling it is in our own struggles to remember that St. Paul also had his struggles. He was not always successful in his ministry, like the poor response he got to his speech in Athens (cf. Acts 17:16-34). St. Paul also had to fight his own interior battles: "For I do not do the good I want, but I do the evil I do not want" (Romans 7:19).

The saints take away our excuses; if they can be holy, why can't we? The saints have come in all shapes and sizes. There are priestly saints, like St. John Vianney, and lay saints, like St. Gianna Beretta Molla. There are saints who were university professors, like St. Thomas Aquinas, and ones who were door keepers, such as St. Andre Bessette. There are saints that died quite old, such as St. Padre Pio, and those who died quite young, such as St. Maria Goretti and St. Dominic Savio. The list could go on. Saints were not without their struggles, and, save the Blessed Mother[a], they were not without their sins or faults. They were ordinary people who loved God and neighbor extraordinarily.

We must also ask the saints to intercede with God for us with their prayers. Just as we pray for each other while on earth, our community with the saints does not end simply because they are in heaven.[69] They may intercede in some practical needs for us – from finding lost items with the help of St. Anthony of Padua to finding a possible spouse with the help of Sts. Anne and Joachim. However, their primary interest would be for us, like them, to eventually make it to heaven.

Not everyone will be officially recognized by the Church as a saint (saint with a big "S" as we colloquially say), but everyone is called to make it to heaven (saint with a small "s"). This is not a competition. With the example and intercession of "the Saints," and the mutual help and prayers of those still on this earthly journey with us, we can make it to heaven.

---

a   From the Catechism: n. 490 'To become the mother of the Savior, Mary "was enriched by God with gifts appropriate to such a role"... n. 491 ... the dogma of the Immaculate Conception confesses, as Pope Pius IX proclaimed in 1854: The most Blessed Virgin Mary was, from the first moment of her conception, by a singular grace and privilege of almighty God and by virtue of the merits of Jesus Christ, Savior of the human race, preserved immune from all stain of original sin.... n. 493 ... By the grace of God Mary remained free of every personal sin her whole life long.'

For Further Reflection:

"Like obedient children, do not act in compliance with the desires of your former ignorance but, as he who called you is holy, be holy yourselves in every aspect of your conduct for it is written, 'Be holy because I [am] holy.'"

1 Peter 1:14-16

Some Questions:

1. Do I ever read the lives of the saints?

2. Do I have a saint whom I particularly admire and relate to? Why am I drawn to him or her?

3. Have I ever asked any saint to intercede on my behalf or on behalf of others?

4. Have I tried to imitate something I observed in the life of a saint?

CHAPTER 13

Share the Passion

I have to watch myself. I am already a talker by nature, but if the subject of riding or pro-cycling comes up, someone's most likely going to get an earful. If a non-cyclist makes a comment about racing being "just riding your bike fast," or – gasp – "boring to watch," I almost cannot hold back. I begin my response with the question, "How much do you want to know?" I usually describe one of the grand tours – explain the stages, the team dynamics, drafting, strategies, the distances and terrains raced, average speeds, the different colored leaders' jerseys – the works. The greatest athletes in the world are engaging in a three-week chess match! What's not to love!?

Even if a skeptic mentions the past doping scandals in pro-cycling's still recent history, I am very quick to mention that much has been done to clean things up and prevent such problems from continuing unchecked.[70] Additionally, a somewhat checkered past does not nullify the inherent beautify of the sport and the great achievements of those who have legitimately won.

When fellow riders and cycling fans get together, it's understandable that riding and the pro-circuit will often be a topic of conversation. I remember having dinner with a riding partner and his family, and I had to check my enthusiasm to not talk exclusively about cycling with him out of deference to his wife and children. When we love someone or something, we cannot help but speak about it. We do not need encouragement to share the passion. We simply speak from the fullness of our hearts.

A Passion for Jesus & His Church

The same should hold with our faith in Jesus Christ and his Church.

We should share the passion in our hearts. Cardinal Cantalamessa in his book on Romans titled Life in Christ compares the epistle's opening lines to a breathless messenger with great news:

> "The runner arriving breathlessly in the town square from the battlefield does not begin by giving an orderly account of the development of events and neither does he waste time on details. He goes straight to the point and in a few words gives the most vital piece of news which everyone is waiting to hear. Explanations can come later. If a battle has been won, he shouts: 'Victory!' and if peace has been made, he shouts: 'Peace!' That is how I remember things the day the Second World War ended. The news 'Armistice! Armistice!' brought by someone returning from the city, flashed from house to house in the town and spread throughout the countryside. The people poured out on to the streets embracing one another with tears in their eyes after the terrible years of war. St. Paul, chosen to announce

the Gospel, behaves in the same way at the beginning of his Letter to the Romans. He comes as the herald of the greatest event in the world, as the messenger of the most splendid of victories and hastens to tell us, in a few words, the most beautiful news ever told: 'To all God's beloved people in Rome'— he says— 'who are called to be saints: Grace to you and peace from God our Father and the Lord Jesus Christ'! (Romans 1:7). At first reading, this might seem just a simple greeting, like those at the beginning of each letter, whereas, in fact, it contains news. And what news! I announce, he is saying, that God loves you; that once and for all peace has been made between heaven and earth; I tell you that you 'have grace'!" [71]

Familiarity with the Gospel message runs the risk of becoming old news rather than Good News. Somewhere along the line routine might have set in so that the faith no longer seems to resonate. "Yeah, I've heard the story already" seems to be the bored response of many a cradle Catholic. The opposite should be true. The more we engage our faith in Jesus and his Church through study, prayer, and service, the more our love for them should grow.

I remember once while not yet ordained, another brother and I were travelling to visit friends of our congregation in northern Italy to promote our work and ask for a donation. We came to one modest but well-kept house. The woman, a grandmother and widow, received us and offered us coffee and pastries, which we gladly accepted. I remember little to nothing of what I said. What I do remember is that several times during our hour-long conversation, our host paused from commenting on the normal challenges faced by a grandmother, glance reflectively upward, and remind us three, "But why worry? God is my Father." She meant it. She lived it, and I still remember our meeting after 20 years. She spoke softly but with the conviction of a deep faith. She knew God. She spoke from the fullness of her heart.

Our enthusiasm must be rooted in a love for God – Father, Son, and Holy Spirit – but it does not stop there. By extension we are called to love Christ's Mystical Body the Church precisely because she is an extension of him, a sacrament of his presence in the world.[72] When we study Catholic theology in some depth we marvel at the logical coherence and beauty of her doctrine. When we contemplate her contributions to Western culture – to philosophy, law, science, economics, and the very institution of the university – we are awestruck.[73] When we read the lives of the saints, we are inspired. How can we not share this with the whole world?

Even the scandals in the Church, while painful, should not keep us from loving the Church. This is no excuse for scandal and cover-up, a plague found in all human institutions. We love the Church not because its members are not sinners – we all are – but because it belongs to Jesus, who is actively at work in the Church. He is busy, slowly but surely, in converting us sinners into saints. The Good News, as St. Paul proclaimed to the Romans, is that we are called to be saints through grace. How can we not share this with the whole world?

For Further Reflection:

"Paul, a slave of Christ Jesus, called to be an apostle and set apart for the Gospel of God, which he promised previously through his prophets in the Holy scriptures, the Gospel about his Son, descended from David according to the flesh, but established as Son of God in power according to the spirit of holiness through Resurrection from the dead, Jesus Christ our Lord. Through him we have received the grace of apostleship, to bring about the obedience of faith, for the sake of his name, among all the Gentiles, among whom are you also, who are called to belong to Jesus Christ: to all the beloved of God in Rome, called to be holy. Grace to you and peace from God our Father and the Lord Jesus Christ."

Romans 1:1-7

Some Questions:

1. How often do I speak about cycling and pro-cycling with friends and acquaintances?

2. How often do I speak about my faith in Jesus Christ?

3. How often do I share the beauty and the truth of the Catholic Church – her doctrine, her history, and her saints?

4. Am I familiar with the Church's doctrine and history?

CHAPTER 14

Enjoy the Ride

A few years back after having preached a particularly long and demanding retreat, I went for a Sunday afternoon bike ride. It was still pretty cold (high 40s); the leaves had not yet returned on the trees, but it was warm enough to ride on the trail by the river. Due to the cold, there were few cyclists and hikers. It seemed I had the trail to myself. It felt good to get on the bike and pray. I saw a cardinal fly past me several times, three appearances by the rare bluebird, and, finally, a buck that crossed my path just a few meters in front of me. It seemed Our Lord was kindly helping me connect with nature and relax. This ride was so memorable because the highlights were not so much my ride per se, but my conversation with God and my encounter with nature all around me.

It's not that I don't enjoy my typical rides. I do, very much so. However, that enjoyment is often achievement-based. By nature, I am intense, so I'm usually trying to beat my previous time on any given ride. I may still take in the scenery and appreciate it, but it will not be my primary focus.

I still remember riding with another priest from my community. After he stopped to "smell the flowers" at least twice within two miles, we agreed to a meeting point and time and went our separate ways. (I did not follow my own advice offered in chapter 2.) Nevertheless, my fellow priest had something that I must not allow my intensity to fully overshadow: it is good to take in the beauty and goodness all around us- in nature and in persons.

Appreciating God's Gifts

"God looked at everything he had made, and found it very good" (Genesis 1:31).

In our life as Christians, or simply as human beings, we can become so goal-oriented – even with holy goals – that we forget to appreciate the joys of every day. If life is a gift from God, then it makes sense that the first thing we must do is accept and appreciate the gift – enjoy life. This is not the same as declaring pleasure to be the most important thing in life. At times we may have to sacrifice pleasure out of love, like staying with a sick relative when we would rather go on a bike ride. Nevertheless, if love is giving, it is also receiving.

So, enjoy the birds singing, the flowers blooming, the sun shining, our child's laughter, and our spouse's affection. Behind all those good things and sustaining them is God's love for us.

That enjoyment and appreciation of the gifts that life brings us will move us to a profound gratitude toward God. One of my favorite poems of gratitude is by one of my favorite persons, the Blessed Mother:

"My soul proclaims the greatness of the Lord; my spirit rejoices in God my Savior. For he has looked upon his handmaid's lowliness; behold, from now on will all ages call me blessed. The Mighty One has done great things for me, and holy is his name. His mercy is from age to age to those who fear him. He has shown might with his arm, dispersed the arrogant of mind and heart. He has thrown down the rulers from their thrones but lifted up the lowly. The hungry he has filled with good things; the rich he has sent away empty. He has helped Israel his servant, remembering his mercy, according to his promise to our fathers, to Abraham and to his descendants forever" (Luke 1:46-55).

Gratitude not only increases the enjoyment, but also our confidence in and love for God. "Look how good God has been to me, how can I not trust and love him more?!"

Recognizing God's gifts and having gratitude for those gifts is perhaps the fastest way to happiness and holiness. So, as we work diligently toward our goals, let's not forget to enjoy the ride along the way.

For Further Reflection:

"I will bless the LORD at all times; his praise shall be always in my mouth. My soul will glory in the LORD; let the poor hear and be glad. Magnify the LORD with me; and let us exalt his name together."

Psalm 34:2-4

Some Questions:

1. How good am I at taking time to "smell the flowers" and enjoy the small things of everyday life?

2. How good am I at making time for relationships? Do I make time for others?

3. How frequently do I thank God for the graces of a given day?

4. How good am at I thanking people for their service, friendship, and love?

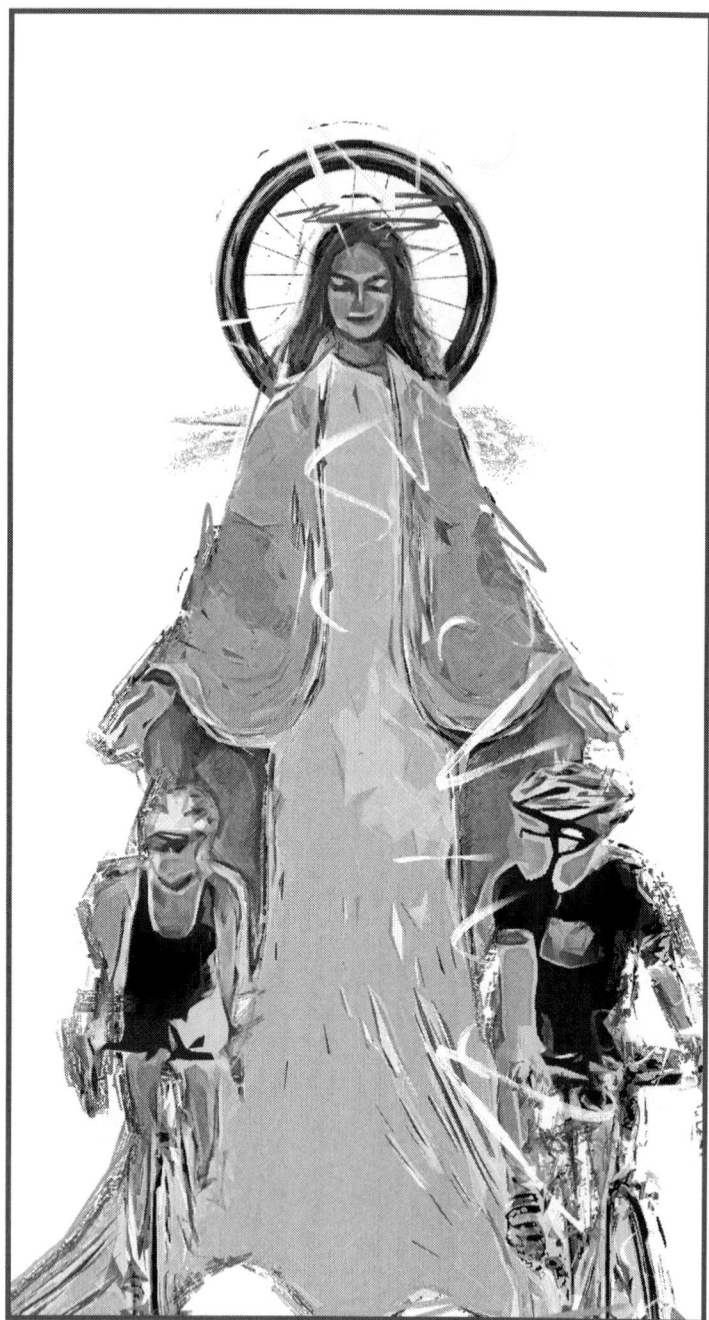

CHAPTER 15

Cycling's Patron & Her Shrine – The Madonna del Ghisallo

Every family needs a mother, even cyclists. The Church has understood this from the time of the Apostles. On the cross Jesus entrusted Mary to John's care and vice versa (cf. John 19:26-27). However, Mary's spiritual maternity was not exclusive to John; all the Apostles had a great esteem for the mother of their Lord. That is why shortly before the coming of the Holy Spirit, the Apostles were gathered with Mary, and other women, in prayer (cf. Acts 1:14). St. John Paul II writes, "Entrusting himself to Mary in a filial manner, the Christian, like the Apostle John, 'welcomes' the Mother of Christ 'into his own home.'"[74]

As Catholics we believe that honoring the Mother of Jesus, and asking for her to pray for us, will only help us draw closer to Jesus, since that is what she did for others her entire earthly life. For example, Mary brought Jesus to Elizabeth and John during the Visitation. She allowed the shepherds and Magi to honor her newborn in Bethlehem. She encouraged the servants to "Do whatever he tells you" at the wedding feast of Cana.[75] Now as we already saw in the chapter on the saints, our relationships with loved ones do not end when they go to Heaven. Therefore, we continue to relate to Mary – our Blessed Mother – in Heaven, asking her to pray for us and to help us get to know her Son better.

Throughout the Church's history there have been numerous apparitions of the Blessed Mother.[a][76] Some of the more renowned ones include Our Lady of Fatima (Portugal in 1917), Our Lady of Lourdes (France in 1858), and Our Lady of Guadalupe (Mexico in 1531), each with its own shrine.

There is however, a lesser-known apparition and shrine that has officially become both the patroness and shrine for cyclists: "The Madonna del Ghisallo" near the shores of Lake Como in northern Italy. Tradition has it that the Count of Ghisallo was in the area, and threatened by bandits. He prayed for help and ran toward an apparition of Mary, who saved him from his attackers.[77] Originally, a church was built there in 1623 and later expanded. Then, as the location became increasingly popular with travelers – especially cyclists – Pope Pius XII named the Madonna del Ghisallo as the patron saint of cyclists in 1949.[78]

So now we have our own patroness and shrine to visit, and if we have the legs to make it up the hill, we can ride to it.[79] The Church itself

"hosts a series of celebratory artworks dedicated to cyclists, both living and deceased. Just in front of its entrance we find two statues depicting the famous Italian riders Gino Bartali and Fausto Coppi, while on the side of the building there is a moving bronze statue titled 'Monument dedicated to a cyclist' built by Elio Ponti in 1973.... In 2006, a fully equipped Museum of Cyclists opened its doors on the scenic terrace just outside the church, with Pope Benedict XVI blessing the final stone, which was inscribed with the words "Omnia Vincit Amor" (Love conquers all).[80]

This fits wonderfully in the Church's tradition of pilgrimages, where believers visit spiritually significant sites on a prayerful journey. One of the more famous pilgrim destinations is Santiago de Compostela (St. James of Compostela) in northwestern corner of Spain. Most pilgrims would visit this on foot, but cycling pilgrims also go. Other well-known shrines include the above-mentioned places of apparition: Fatima, Lourdes, and Our Lady of Guadalupe. Another famous destination is Our Lady of Czestochowa, a beloved destination of St. John Paul II.

How wonderful it would be to pick a spiritual destination and, after assuring that our route is safe, organize a group for a cycling pilgrimage.

(If you need a chaplain for that pilgrimage, let me know.)

For Further Reflection:

"Each year his parents went to Jerusalem for the feast of Passover, and when he was twelve years old, they went up according to festival custom. After they had completed its days, as they were returning, the boy Jesus remained behind in Jerusalem, but his parents did not know it. Thinking that he was in the caravan, they journeyed for a day and looked for him among their relatives and acquaintances, but not finding him, they returned to Jerusalem to look for him. After three days they found him in the temple, sitting in the midst of the teachers, listening to them and asking them questions, and all who heard him were astounded at his understanding and his answers. When his parents saw him, they were astonished, and his mother said to him, 'Son, why have you done this to us? Your father and I have been looking for you with great anxiety.' And he said to them, 'Why were you looking for me? Did you not know that I must be in my Father's house?' But they did not understand what he said to them. He went down with them and came to Nazareth, and was obedient to them; and his mother kept all these things in her heart. And Jesus advanced [in] wisdom and age and favor before God and man."

Luke 2:41-52

Some Questions:

1. Have you ever been on a pilgrimage? Were you able to go, at least in part, by foot or bike?

2. What are some of the sites you would like to visit? Why? What spiritual significance does that particular location have for you?

3. How is your relationship with the Blessed Mother?

CHAPTER 16

Do We Have Another Patron Saint for Cycling? Gino Bartali

Gino Bartali was born in 1914 in the town of Ponte Emma near Florence, Italy, the firstborn of a poor day laborer. He led a humble but happy childhood, like most of the boys from his town. However, when it was time for him to go to the sixth grade at age 11, he would need a bicycle to get to school. After working a summer job for a farmer, he was able to save up enough to buy a second-hand bicycle. He was in love. Not much later, Gino and his younger brother by about two years, Giulio, would ride with friends around the hills near their home having impromptu races. As he got older, it became evident that Gino had talent. There was however one big obstacle to Gino racing; his parents were adamantly opposed to it. Cycling could be a dangerous sport. However, after some time, Gino's father reluctantly agreed to let him race.[81]

Rather quickly, Gino established himself as a promising young professional and began winning races. With success came money – eventually enough to buy his parents a nicer house – and fame. One of the few people who could keep up with Gino on the bike was actually his younger brother, Giulio, who himself had begun racing as an amateur. Then in 1936 tragedy struck. During a race, Giulio crashed into a car and died shortly after.[82] Gino went into a serious depression and withdrew from racing and, really, the rest of the world. Only after some time and with the persuasion of his then future wife, Adriana, did Gino begin to race again. She told him to honor Giulio's memory by racing.[83] The tragedy was also fundamental in Gino turning more profoundly to his Catholic faith, something he maintained for the rest of his life.[84]

Upon his return to racing, Gino continued to succeed. By 1938, and at only 24 years old, Gino had already won the Italian National Championships twice, the Giro d'Italia general classification twice, countless one-day races, and most importantly, the Tour de France.[85] However, the Second Word War interrupted all the major races shortly thereafter, just when Gino was at the prime of his racing career.[86]

Eventually conscripted into the Italian Army, Gino was made a bike messenger, which allowed him to continue training.[87] Then in 1943, at the invitation of Cardinal Elia Dalla Costa of Florence, Gino became part of a network which created fake identification documents to help Jews to escape Fascist capture. Gino served as a courier to transport the documents by hiding them beneath his seat post within the frame of his bike. No one would suspect the famous cyclist when on a training ride. Had he been caught, however, the price would have likely been imprisonment and death. Not even his wife could know of his missions.[88] This service to the Jewish community only came to light years after the War, and even then, Gino was reluctant to talk about it.[89] However, in 2013, 13 years after his death,

Israel's Official Holocaust Memorial, Yad Vashem, named Gino "Righteous Among the Nations."[90]

Once the war ended, Italy, and all of Europe, had the difficult task of rebuilding. Naturally, it took professional cycling time to do the same. Nevertheless, it did, and the Tour de France restarted in 1947. Gino, however, would not compete in it until the following year.[91]

The 1948 Tour took place at a particularly tense moment in Italy. In 1946 there had been a strongly divisive election primarily among the Christian Democrats, the Communists, and the Socialists.[92] While the Christian Democrats won, there was still great tension between the political factions. Then, during the Tour, in which Gino had fallen behind, the Italian Communist leader, Palmiro Togliatti, was shot three times in Rome and was in danger of dying.[93] Riots and tensions were breaking out throughout the country. There was even a fisticuff in Parliament. Under a great deal of pressure, the Christian Democratic Parliamentary President, Alcide de Gasperi, called his old friend from Catholic circles, Gino.[94] He told Gino that "Italy needed Bartali to do what he best knew how to do, to win stage races."[95] At already 16 minutes behind the overall leader, and having struggled to that point, it was a big ask. Nevertheless, Gino raced two subsequent mountain stages that can only be called "inspired." After those two stages he took the yellow jersey[a] and held onto it to take the overall win.[96]

"Just as it seemed the communists would stage a full-scale revolt, a deputy ran into the chamber shouting 'Bartali's

---

a   Yellow Jersey — It is the jersey of the over-all leader of the Tour de France in its general classification.

won the Tour de France!' All differences were at once forgotten as the feuding politicians applauded and congratulated each other on a cause for such national pride. That day, with immaculate timing, Togliatti awoke from his coma on his hospital bed, inquired how the Tour was going, and recommended calm. All over the country political animosities were for the time being swept aside by the celebrations and a looming crisis was averted... [Later, one politician commented,] 'To say that civil war was averted by a Tour de France victory is surely excessive. But it is undeniable that... Bartali contributed to easing the tensions.'"[97]

Gino competed in the following Tour in 1949 and took second place to Fausto Coppi, his archrival in cycling. Remarkably, the two worked together in this Tour.[98] The rivalry between the two was usually so intense that during the 1948 World Championship, in which they were both on the same national team, they both got off their bikes rather than help each other. Consequently, both were suspended by the Italian Cycling Association for two months.[99] Followers of either Bartali or Coppi throughout Italy took their allegiance very seriously.[100] However, there is a famous photo of the two sharing a water bottle in the 1952 Tour.[101]

Gino retired from cycling at the age of 40.[102] Afterwards, he attempted several business endeavors with minimal success.[103] He died in 2000 at the age of 85 leaving behind his wife, two sons, and a daughter.[104]

Was he a saint? Could he be canonized some day? I cannot say. We must not overlook his human shortcomings, such as his competitiveness to the point of being petty at times – like when he would sneak into the rooms of competitors to see if they were taking performance enhancing drugs.[105] [106] Nevertheless, Gino was nicknamed "Gino the Pious"[107] (among other, less flattering, nicknames), was sincerely religious, and refused to hide his Catholic devotion even when it was discouraged under the Fascist regime and was a risk to his career.[108]

Regardless of any possible future canonization, I believe that Gino Bartali is a saint with a small "s" (in heaven). He is a personal hero of mine, on and off the bike, and I will ask him to pray for me to be both a good rider and a good person.

For Further Reflection:

"[But] take care not to perform righteous deeds in order that people may see them; otherwise, you will have no recompense from your heavenly Father. When you give alms, do not blow a trumpet before you, as the hypocrites do in the synagogues and in the streets to win the praise of others. Amen, I say to you, they have received their reward. But when you give alms, do not let your left hand know what your right is doing, so that your almsgiving may be secret. And your Father who sees in secret will repay you."

Matthew 6:1-4

Some Questions:

1. How often do I intentionally seek to help others in need?

2. How discrete am I with my charity, whether it be financial or practical?

3. How could my particular talents – cycling or otherwise – contribute in a unique way to helping others?

4. How good am I at recognizing and appreciating the services others provide for me?

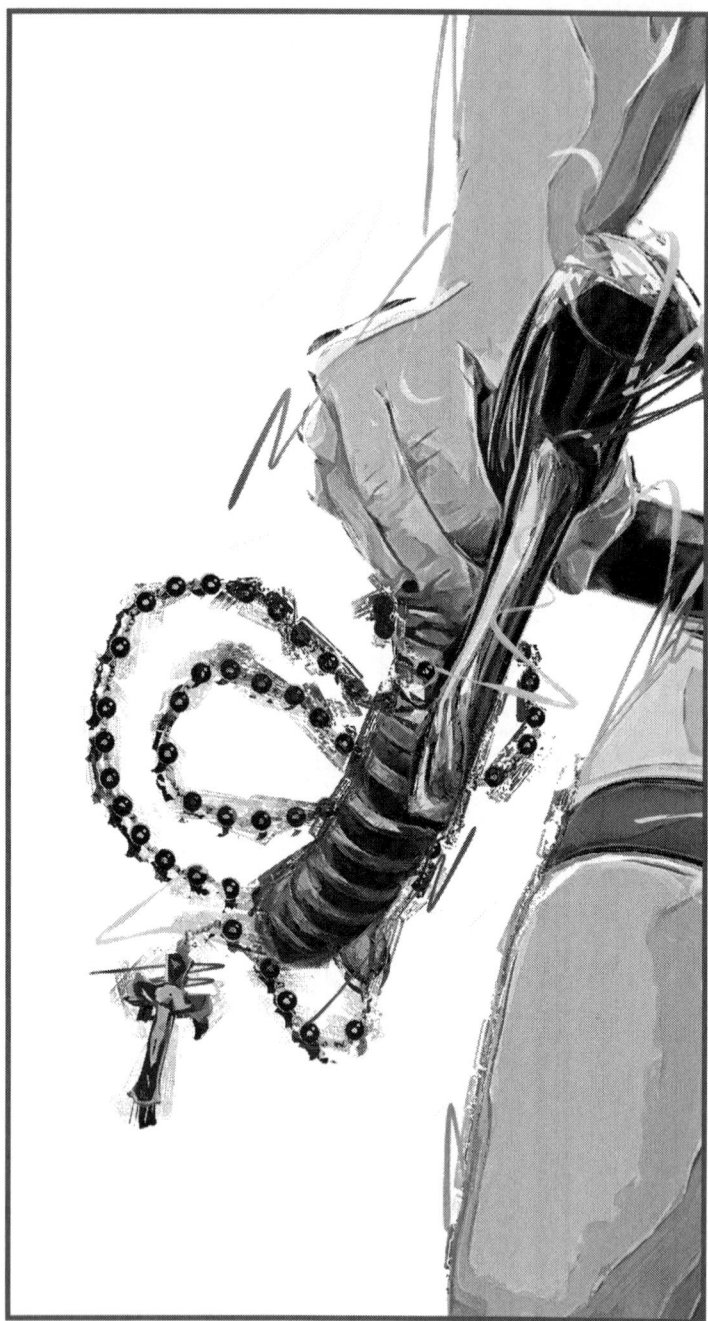

CHAPTER 17

Praying the Rosary on the Bike

Ideas attract me. I enjoy philosophy, theology (no surprise there), literature, art, and current events. I try to reflect and discern what God is doing in the world and what he is asking of me. But it is hard for me to give my mind a rest. It is probably one of the primary reasons I enjoy cycling and praying the rosary, which I frequently do together. Both bring me peace, and I find the combination powerful.

An intense ride brings a degree of interior peace because afterward, and at times during, we are simply too fatigued to be overly stressed. We get out the nervous energy; we're spent.

Now, I will usually spend part of my ride listening to an audiobook (I can't stop thinking altogether). Even then, the book is frequently more for enjoyment (fiction) rather than study. And yes, I will also listen to music during the ride, usually fast-paced classical pieces like Dvorak's Ninth Symphony to help me keep a good cadence.

However, I believe my most fruitful and peaceful moments on the bike are when I pray. Now there are many ways to pray on the bike – just not with our eyes closed. At times I will do a conscience exam – a conversation with Christ to see if I have been living my day according to his will for me. At times I simply converse with Our Lord. At other times I contemplate the beauty of nature around me and praise him for such a gift. I even take moments to thank him for the gift of riding (which I should do more often).

Interestingly enough, while I can focus rather intensely at times, at other times I find myself easily distracted – even during prayer. It was on my bike that I noticed that the rosary can be very good for us distracted types. More on this in a moment.

However, first I would like to reflect on the purpose of the rosary per se. Why do Catholics pray the rosary? Does it distract us from the centrality of Christ by paying too much attention to Mary?

The Glossary of the Catechism defines the rosary as:
> "A prayer in honor of the Blessed Virgin Mary, which repeats the privileged Marian prayer… Hail Mary, in 'decades' of ten prayers, each preceded by the… Our Father… and concluded by the… Glory Be to the Father…, accompanied by meditation on the mysteries of Christ's life. The rosary was developed by medieval piety in the Latin church as a popular substitute for the liturgical prayer of the Hours."[109]

Now the Church holds that we should rightly honor the Blessed Mother, but that this devotion "differs essentially from the adoration which is given to the incarnate Word and equally to the Father and the Holy Spirit, and greatly fosters this adoration." [110] As stated in a previous chapter, our relationship with Mary is meant to bring us closer to Jesus.

The rosary is no different. It is ultimately meant to be a meditation on the different "mysteries" of the life of Christ.[111] Each of the four sets of mysteries present five events from the life of Christ. For example, the Joyful Mysteries reflect upon his childhood. The Luminous Mysteries reflect upon Jesus's public life. The Sorrowful Mysteries reflect on his Passion. The Glorious Mysteries reflect upon his Resurrection and beyond.

For our prayer to be most fruitful, we are supposed to focus on those mysteries while we pray. If we contemplate or "see" the mysteries of Christ, the "Hail Marys" are like the background music or the soundtrack to our contemplation to help keep us focused. Additionally, I find the repetition of the prayers soothing, which can also aid contemplation – if I don't fall asleep (a nonissue on the bike).

What I learned on the bike is that since I am easily distracted, I can quickly get sidetracked in my simple conversations with Our Lord, and think about completely different topics. Holding the beads and praying the "Hail Marys" remind me in my most distracted moments that I am trying to pray. This can renew my attention to return to meditation. Another way to pray the rosary is to simply concentrate on the words of the prayers, as we would with any vocal prayer.[a] Finally, I have to believe that one's desire to pray, even with distractions, has value to Our Lord; otherwise, we can fall into the trap of perfectionism.

Praying the rosary is a wonderful way to grow closer to Christ and his Mother; I encourage anyone not in the habit to try it.

---

a   Vocal prayer – a pre-written prayer with which the person tries to identify with the words being said, such as the "Our Father."

We can start by simply praying one mystery daily – and then go from there. And yes, we should try praying the rosary while we ride.

(Wrap the rosary beads around the brake lever while praying to avoid dropping them.)

For Further Reflection:

"In the sixth month, the angel Gabriel was sent from God to a town of Galilee called Nazareth, to a virgin betrothed to a man named Joseph, of the house of David, and the virgin's name was Mary. And coming to her, he said, 'Hail, favored one! The Lord is with you.' But she was greatly troubled at what was said and pondered what sort of greeting this might be. Then the angel said to her, 'Do not be afraid, Mary, for you have found favor with God. Behold, you will conceive in your womb and bear a son, and you shall name him Jesus. He will be great and will be called Son of the Most High, and the Lord God will give him the throne of David his father, and he will rule over the house of Jacob forever, and of his kingdom there will be no end.' But Mary said to the angel, 'How can this be, since I have no relations with a man?' And the angel said to her in reply, 'The Holy Spirit will come upon you, and the power of the Most High will overshadow you. Therefore the child to be born will be called holy, the Son of God.'"

Luke 1:26-35

"When Elizabeth heard Mary's greeting, the infant leaped in her womb, and Elizabeth, filled with the Holy Spirit, cried out in a loud voice and said, 'Most blessed are you among women, and blessed is the fruit of your womb. And how does this happen to me, that the mother of my Lord should come to me?'"

Luke 1:41-43

Some Questions:

1. Do I understand and appreciate my relationship with Mary? How do I relate to her?

2. Do I understand my relationship with Mary as a fruitful way to know Jesus better?

3. Do I pray the rosary either individually or with my family?

CHAPTER 18

Giving Witness on the Bike

Every Catholic, every Christian, is called to proclaim Christ by the testimony of one's life and with one's word.[112] This obligation would hold in all the different aspects of a person's life – including cycling. What would that look like?

Let's start with our most common experience, a training ride on the road or on the trail. If we are alone on our ride, there is perhaps relatively little to be done. However, small gestures matter.

For example, we can be courteous, even when people inadvertently force us to slow down. We can greet everyone along the way with a word or even a simple nod. In addition to warning people that we are coming behind them – "on your left" – we might add "have a good one," or even "God bless." One year I rode on Easter Sunday, and made a point of wishing others a "happy Easter." Many, not all, responded in kind.

Additionally, we can have something on our person or on our bike that shows that we are Christian. I usually have my necklace with the Crucifix and the Miraculous Medal outside of my jersey. The other priests in my community bought me a jersey with the Cross on it, which I wear from time to time.

I frequently have rosary beads in my hand while praying, or simply have them wrapped around the brake lever when not.

If we are riding in a group, there may be opportunities to share the faith with them. Since behavior often speaks louder than words, we must be willing to pull our fair share – or more. We must also be willing to be pulled if needed. We can bring extra snacks and gels to share, encourage the others when they seem fatigued, or wait for them if needed. If the ride is not too intense and conversation is possible, we may want to talk about the faith, or even invite them to pray briefly with us.

We might organize a local biking pilgrimage for some friends. Is there a church, chapel, or statue of Jesus, Mary, or another saint within a safe trajectory from our bike route? The group might ride there, stop to pray, and then ride back. This could be a few friends one Saturday or a full-blown event with a ride, prayer, possible Mass, and closing meal. We must be careful yet creative.

For Further Reflection:

"You are the salt of the earth. But if salt loses its taste, with what can it be seasoned? It is no longer good for anything but to be thrown out and trampled underfoot. You are the light of the world. A city set on a mountain cannot be hidden. Nor do they light a lamp and then put it under a bushel basket; it is set on a lampstand, where it gives light to all in the house. Just so, your light must shine before others, that they may see your good deeds and glorify your heavenly Father."

Matthew 5:13-16

Some Questions:

1. How willing or hesitant am I to let others know that I am Catholic?

2. Do I ever speak about my faith to others?

3. Have I ever found a feasible way of sharing my faith with others in the cycling community?

CHAPTER 19

Offering It Up

Serious cycling hurts. Make sure that that built-in sacrifice does not go without spiritually tapping into it.

The Church has a long tradition of seeing sacrifice as a wonderful opportunity to love God and neighbor. Why? Love is essentially a giving of oneself, a spending oneself for the good of the other. The expectant mother nourishes her child from her very substance. The father works hard to provide for and protect the family. The pastor of a parish is busy spiritually attending his community. Real love is not without sacrifice.

While we may grasp that practical sacrifice is necessary to fulfill one's duty or be charitable, we may question why sacrifice by itself does anyone any good.

When we unite our sacrifices to Christ's redemptive suffering, our suffering takes on a supernatural meaning. In a small way we collaborate in Christ's salvific work. This is the very purpose of the offertory during the Mass.[113] When people bring up the gifts of bread and wine, they represent all their efforts from daily life – all the struggles and victories. They are offered to Christ so that he can insert them into his own self-offering to the Father in the Passion. In turn, Jesus offers us his Body and Blood in the Eucharist so that we have the strength to keep going.

Therefore, our sacrifices can have a supernatural value when offered to God out of love. However, we must take care that our sacrifices are not detrimental to our health or our responsibilities. Just as we must exercise moderation in cycling, so too in sacrifice.

Finally, similar to prayer, we may offer the sacrifice for a particular intention – like the well-being or conversion of a loved one.

So, the next time we push just a bit harder to beat our previous best time, we can remember to offer it to Christ as a small sacrifice of love.

For Further Reflection:

"The Jewish feast of Passover was near. When Jesus raised his eyes and saw that a large crowd was coming to him, he said to Philip, 'Where can we buy enough food for them to eat?' He said this to test him, because he himself knew what he was going to do. Philip answered him, 'Two hundred days' wages worth of food would not be enough for each of them to have a little [bit].' One of his disciples, Andrew, the brother of Simon Peter, said to him, 'There is a boy here who has five barley loaves and two fish; but what good are these for so many?' Jesus said, 'Have the people recline.' Now there was a great deal of grass in that place. So the men reclined, about five thousand in number. Then Jesus took the loaves, gave thanks, and distributed them to those who were reclining, and also as much of the fish as they wanted. When they had had their fill, he said to his disciples, 'Gather the fragments left over, so that nothing will be wasted.'"

John 6:4-12

Some Questions:

1. How sacrificial am I in simply fulfilling my duty? Do I recognize this as the most important sacrifice?

2. Do I ever "supernaturalize" my sacrifices offering them to God?

3. Is my participation in Mass an intentional and active self-offering of all that I am to God?

Conclusion

Those who have read this far in the booklet clearly share a similar passion for Jesus and for cycling as I do. While Jesus takes priority, I believe that he allows us the gift of cycling in our lives for a reason. Ultimately, like all created things, cycling must somehow contribute to making us better disciples of Jesus. This booklet has attempted to reflect on some of the spiritual lessons we can learn from cycling and some of the ways we can bring Christ with us on our rides.

I pray that we all continue to have a fruitful journey – on the bike and with the Lord.

May God bless us, and keep pedaling.

Recommended Reading

This booklet has been a simple reflection on cycling and the faith. However, it does touch upon several themes from our Catholic faith. Perhaps readers would like to deepen their knowledge on some of those themes. I would encourage it.

Below are some books I recommend, sorted according to broad themes.

Church Teaching

- Compendium of the Catechism of the Catholic Church. United States Conference of Catholic Bishops Washington DC: USCCB. 2006. (A short version of the Catholic Catechism. It's a great overview of the faith in a succinct manner.)

- A Map of Life: A Simple Study of the Catholic Faith. Frank Sheed. San Francisco: Ignatius Press. 1994. (Originally published in 1933.) (A more philosophical approach to the basic truths of the faith.)

- Being Catholic: What Every Catholic Should Know. Suzie Andres. San Francisco: Ignatius Press (with Augustine Institute). 2020. (Focuses on doctrines, customs, traditions, and practices of the Church.)

- God and the World: Believing and Living in Our Time. A Conversation with Peter Seewald. Joseph Cardinal Ratzinger. Translated by Henry Taylor. San Francisco: Ignatius Press. 2002. (A fascinating interview with Cardinal Ratzinger [Pope Benedict XVI] regarding countless issues facing the Church.) The Mass & the Eucharist

The Mass & the Eucharist

- <u>Know Him in the Breaking of the Bread</u>. Fr. Francis Randolph. San Francisco: Ignatius Press. 2011. (An accessible explanation of the meaning of the Mass.)

- <u>Bread That Is Broken</u>. Fr. Wilfrid Stinissen, OCD. Translated by Sr. Clare Marie, OCD. San Francisco: Ignatius Press. 2020. (A reflection on the centrality of the Eucharist and the need to cherish such a gift.)

The Bible

- <u>Inside the Bible: An Introduction to Each Book of the Bible</u>. Fr. Kenneth Baker, SJ. San Francisco: Ignatius Press. 1998. (An introduction to each book of the Bible to help the reader grow in knowledge of the Bible.)

- <u>The Better Part: A Christ-Centered Resource for Personal Prayer</u>. Fr. John Bartunek, LC, STHD. Algonquin, Illinois: Ministry23, LLC. 2014. (Reflections on all four Gospels, passage by passage, with an introduction on how to pray.)

The Blessed Mother

- <u>The World's First Love: Mary, Mother of God</u>. Archbishop Fulton Sheen. San Francisco: Ignatius Press. 2010. (Originally published in 1952.) (Archbishop Sheen's reflection on the Blessed Virgin Mary.)

- Behold Your Mother: A Biblical and Historical Defense of the Marian Doctrines. Tim Staples. El Cajon, California: Catholic Answers. 2014. (Explanation of the Church's teaching on the Blessed Virgin Mary.)

- Handmaid of the Lord. Adrienne von Speyr. San Francisco: Ignatius Press. 2017. (Reflections on the inner life of the Blessed Mother.)

- Praying the Rosary Like Never Before: Encounter the Wonder of Heaven and Earth. Edward Sri. Cincinnati, Ohio: Servant. 2017. (Explanation of the rosary and the devotion to Mary as well as offering practical tips on praying the rosary.)

The Saints

- Heroism and Genius: How Catholic Priests Helped Build—and Can Help Rebuild—Western Civilization. William J Slattery. San Francisco: Ignatius Press. 2017. (An overview of countless times Catholic bishops and priests have contributed powerfully to Western culture.)

- Confessions of St. Augustine – Ignatius Critical Editions (with Commentary by Fr. David V. Meconi). San Francisco: Ignatius Press. 2012. (Perhaps the most well-known conversion story by a saint.)

- Married Saints and Blesseds Through the Centuries. Ferdinand Holboeck. San Francisco: Ignatius Press. 2002. (Stories of lay saints.)

Suffering

- The Problem of Pain. C. S. Lewis. New York: Harper Collins. 2001. (Originally published in 1940.) (The most famous Christian apologist of the 20th Century tries to respond to the age-old question of how a good God allows for suffering.)

- Arise from Darkness: What to Do When Life Doesn't Make Sense. Benedict Groeschel, CFR. San Francisco: Ignatius Press. 1995. (Priest & psychologist, Fr. Groeschel reflects on his years of accompanying others in their suffering.)

- Now and Forever: A Regnum Christi Essay on an Approach to Living Life in Light of Eternity. Fr. Daniel Brandenburg, LC. RC Spirituality Center. 2021. (Having suffered severe health issues, Fr. Daniel reflects on the meaning of life in light of eternity.)

Seeking Peace

- The Ruthless Elimination of Hurry. John Mark Comer. Colorado Springs, Colorado: WaterBrook. 2019. (A Protestant pastor burns out, learns to slow down, and shares his insights.)

- Interior Freedom. Fr. Jacques Philippe. Translated by Helena Scott. New York: New York. Scepter Publishers. 2007. (What do we have to do to achieve an interior freedom and peace?)

The Spiritual Life

- Introduction to the Devout Life. St. Francis De Sales. San Francisco: Ignatius Press. 2015. (Originally published in 1609.) (A classic which teaches us how to pursue holiness in a very practical manner.)

- Life in Christ. Cardinal Raniero Cantalamessa, translated by Frances Lonergan. Collegeville, Minnesota: Liturgical Press. 1997. (A beautiful meditation on the spiritual themes introduced in St. Paul's Letter to the Romans.)

Conversion Stories

- Rome Sweet Home: Our Journey to Catholicism. Scott & Kimberly Hahn. San Francisco: Ignatius Press. 1993. (An Evangelical pastor and his wife's journey into the Catholic Church.)

- From Atheism to Catholicism. Brandon McGinley, Ed. Irondale, Alabama: EWTN Publishing, Inc. 2017. (A collection of conversion stories from atheism to Catholicism.)

Formation & Personal Growth

- Christin Self-Mastery: How to Govern Your Thoughts, Discipline Your Will, and Achieve Balance in Your Spiritual Life. Basil W. Maturin. Manchester, New Hampshire: Sophia Press. 2001. (Originally published in 1939.) (A study on the importance of virtue and self-control in our lives.)

- Until Christ Be Formed in You: A Regnum Christi Essay on Our Approach to Formation in the Movement. Fr. Daniel Brandenburg, LC. RC Spirituality Center. 2017. (An explanation of integrally forming the whole person as done within the Regnum Christi Movement.)

- The Heart of Virtue. Donald DeMarco. San Francisco: Ignatius Press. 1996. (The importance of forming virtues.)

- A Heart Like Jesus. A Regnum Christi Essay on Contemplating and Imitating Jesus. Fr. John Bullock, LC. RC Spirituality Center. 2020. (A study on going from contemplating the person of Jesus to imitating him... a great read.)

Sharing the Faith

- How to Defend the Faith without Raising Your Voice: Civil Responses to Catholic Hot Button Issues. Austen Ivereigh, Huntington, Indiana: Our Sunday Visitor. 2012. (A useful guide on how to calmly and rationally share the faith – even with polemical topics.)

- The Missionary of Wall Street: From Managing Money to Saving Souls on the Streets of New York. Stephen Auth. Manchester, New Hampshire: Sophia Press. 2019. (A testimony of a financier evangelizing in New York.)

- Catholic Street Evangelization: Stories of Conversion and Witness. Steve Dawson, Ed. San Francisco: Ignatius Press. 2016.(A collection of inspirational stories of conversion and witness.)

Living Charity

- Brother John: A Monk, a Pilgrim and the Purpose of Life. August Turak. Franklin, Tennessee: Clovercroft Publishing. 2018. (A brief and touching story of the power of charity as lived by a Trappist monk.)

- Sharpening Your Tongue: A Regnum Christi Essay on Charity in Our Words. Fr. John Bartunek, LC. STHD. RC Spirituality Center. 2016. (An exhortation with concrete tips on how to live charity in speech.)

Gino Bartali

- Road to Valor: A True Story of World War II Italy, the Nazis, and the Cyclist Who Inspired a Nation. Aili & Andres McConnon.

New York: Crown Publishers. 2012. (A thorough study of the cyclist, Catholic, and hero – particularly good for cycling fans.)

Pilgrimage

- <u>Hiking the Camino: 500 Miles with Jesus</u>. Fr. Dave Pivonka, T.O.R. Cincinnati, OH: Servant Books, 2009. (A collection of meditations on Fr. Dave's pilgrimage on the famous Camino de Santiago.)

Acknowledgements

I want to thank:

Josh Miller, Julia Hoyda, Donna Garrett, Maribeth Harper, Doug Dobrozsi, and Paula Baranecheia for reviewing the text and offering encouragement, suggestions, and numerous corrections.

Fr. Nathaniel Haslam, LC, and Donna Garrett for offering advice on self-publishing.

Mary Ruth Yao for such a professional job of reviewing and copy editing the text.

Paul Latino for the great artwork and promotion.

Deb Levy for help with formatting.

Anthony Grijalva, Jock Pool, and an anonymous donor for financially supporting the project.

Fr. Nikola Derpich, LC for theologically reviewing the text.

God for his constant benevolence and mercy with me, on and off the bike.

Endnotes

1   cf. Romans 5:18.

2   https://blog.littleflower.org/st-therese-daily-devotional/in-his-arms/.

3   cf. Libreria Editrice Vaticana. Catechism of the Catholic Church (Kindle Location 1617). United States Conference of Catholic Bishops. Kindle Edition, n. 162.

4   cf. Froome, Chris. The Climb: The Autobiography (pp. 191-192). Penguin Books Ltd. Kindle Edition.

5   Joseph Cardinal Ratzinger. God and the World: Believing and Living in Our Time. A Conversation with Peter Seewald. Translated by Henry Taylor. San Francisco: Ignatius Press. 2002. 279.

6   Cf. John 3:1-20; Mark 4:1-9; John 18:33-38.

7   Joseph Cardinal Ratzinger. God and the World Believing and Living in Our Time A Conversation with Peter Seewald Translated by Henry Taylor San Francisco: Ignatius Press, 110.

8   Libreria Editrice Vaticana. Catechism of the Catholic Church. United States Conference of Catholic Bishops. Kindle Edition., n. 751.

9   Joseph Cardinal Ratzinger. God and the World..., 68.

10   Cf. https://en.wikipedia.org/wiki/Drafting_(aerodynamics).

11   cf. Global Cycling Network. "How To Draft Like a Pro. Essential Cycling Skills." Feb. 22, 2017 https://youtu.be/fqLdeLchqYA.

12 "TIPS FROM THE PROS: THREE RULES FOR RIDING IN CROSSWINDS" by DANE CASH in Cycling Tips. February 25, 2019. https://cyclingtips.com/2019/02/tips-from-the-pros-three-rules-for-riding-in-crosswinds/.

13 https://en.wikipedia.org/wiki/Team_time_trial.

14 Libreria Editrice Vaticana. Catechism of the Catholic Church (Kindle Location 1617). United States Conference of Catholic Bishops. Kindle Edition, n. 2447.

15 John 13:15.

16 Libreria Editrice Vaticana. Catechism of the Catholic Church (Kindle Location 1617). United States Conference of Catholic Bishops. Kindle Edition, n. 1812.

17 Ibid., n. 1817.

18 "The Actual Effect of Weight on Cycling Speed" in Ride Far, May 2021. https://ridefar.info/bike/cycling-speed/weight/.

19 "How Much Should Road Bikes Weigh?" in Road Bike Basics, https://roadbikebasics.com/how-much-road-bikes-weigh/.

20 cf. Trent Horn & Catherine Pakaluk. Can a Catholic be a Socialist?: The Answer is No – Here's Why. El Cajon, California: Catholic Answers. 2019, 43-46.

21 cf. "How to Fuel for Cycling/Bike Ride Nutrition Explained," Global Cycling Network on YouTube, April 24, 2019. https://www.youtube.com/watch?v=sjhSm3lguxc.

22 cf. Ibid.

23 cf. Ibid.

24 "Dei Verbum." Second Vatican Council. November 18, 1965, n. 25. https://www.vatican.va/archive/hist_councils/ii_vatican_council/documents/vat-ii_const_19651118_dei-verbum_en.html.

25 cf. Libreria Editrice Vaticana. Catechism of the Catholic Church (Kindle Location 1617). United States Conference of Catholic Bishops. Kindle Edition, n. 2559.

26 Ibid., n. 1374.

27 John 6:51.

28 cf. Libreria Editrice Vaticana. Catechism of the Catholic Church (Kindle Location 1617). United States Conference of Catholic Bishops. Kindle Edition, n. 1385.

29 cf. "How the Tour de France Riders Train" by Danielle Kosecki in Bicycling. Aug. 24, 2020. https://www.bicycling.com/tour-de-france/a28355159/how-tour-de-france-riders-train/.

30 Cf. Ibid.

31 Cf. Ibid.

32 "Marginal Gains – Employing the Rule of 1 Percent." Tom Flatau. In TWI – Neuroscience for Business Training that Transforms. October 18, 2019. https://team-working.com/marginal-gains/.

33 "Root Sin Classification... Which One Is Right?" by Fr. John Bartunek, LC, in Spiritual Direction.Com. https://spiritualdirection.com/2010/05/10/root-sin-classifications-which-one-is-right.

34 Cf. Ibid.

35 Cf. Ibid.

36 "What is High-Intensity Interval Training (HIIT)?" Charlie Allenby in Bike Radar. January 18, 2021. https://www.bikeradar.com/advice/fitness-and-training/hiit-interval-training/.

37 Cf. "How the Tour de France Riders Train" by Danielle Kosecki in Bicycling. Aug. 24, 2020. https://www.bicycling.com/tour-de-france/a28355159/how-tour-de-france-riders-train/.

38 cf. "Cycling Power Zones: Training Zones Explained." In Trainer Road Training Blog. Sean Hurley. May 14, 2021. https://www.trainerroad.com/blog/cycling-power-zones-training-zones-explained/.

39 cf. "What is High-Intensity Interval Training (HIIT)?" Charlie Allenby in Bike Radar. January 18, 2021. https://www.bikeradar.com/advice/fitness-and-training/hiit-interval-training/.

40 Jordan Peterson. 12 Rules for Life: An Antidote to Chaos. Toronto: Random House Canada. 2018, 86.

41 cf. Libreria Editrice Vaticana. Catechism of the Catholic Church (Kindle Location 1617). United States Conference of Catholic Bishops. Kindle Edition, n. 2848.

42 Ibid., n. 2848 (quoting 1 Corinthians 10:13).

43 cf. Ibid., n. 307-311.

44 cf. Ibid., n. 2847.

45 Ibid., n. 2847.

46 "Chris Froome 'rammed on purpose' by driver and his bike is severely damaged" in Cycling Weekly, May 9, 2017. https://www.cyclingweekly.com/news/latest-news/chris-froome-rammed-driver-bike-damaged-329461.

47 Ibid.

48 "Wrong-Way Driver Hits Giant-Alpecin Team: Six Riders on Worldtour Team Injured in Training-Camp Crash." By Joe Lindsey. January 24, 2016. https://www.bicycling.com/racing/a20009740/wrong-way-driver-hits-giant-alpecin-team/.

49 'Is the Occasion of Sin a Sin? Roman Catholic Spiritual Direction. In Catholic Exchange by Fr. John Bartunek, LC. June 28,2018. https://catholicexchange.com/occasion-sin-sin/

50 Ibid.

51 cf. Richert, Scott P. "Definition and Examples of an Occasion of Sin." Learn Religions, Aug. 28, 2020, learnreligions.com/what-is-an-occasion-of-sin-542108.

52 cf. Ibid.

54 cf. Ibid

55 cf. Libreria Editrice Vaticana. Catechism of the Catholic Church (Kindle Location 1617). United States Conference of Catholic Bishops. Kindle Edition, n. 1857.

56 Ibid., n. 1858.

56 Ibid., n.1855.

57 Ibid., n.1855.

58 cf. Ibid., n. 1441.

59 Ibid., n. 1456.

60 Ibid., n. 1458..

61 Cf. Ibid., n. 1457

62 DeMarco, Dr. Donald, PhD, New Perspectives on Contraception. One More Soul: Dayton, OH. 1999, 75-76.

63 cf. Libreria Editrice Vaticana. Catechism of the Catholic Church (Kindle Location 1617). United States Conference of Catholic Bishops. Kindle Edition, n. 1785.

64 'Domestique' in Wikipedia. https://en.wikipedia.org/wiki/Domestique

65 cf. 'Dying and Rising on the 2018 Tour de France' in the National Catholic Register by K. V. Turley, August 18, 2018. HTTP://WWW.NCREGISTER.COM/BLOG/KTURLEY/DYING-AND-RISING-ON-THE-2018-TOUR-DE-FRANCE.

66 cf. Ibid.

67 cf. 'Winning Bicycle Racing Illustrated' in Wikipedia. https://en.wikipedia.org/wiki/Winning_Bicycle_Racing_Illustrated.

68 "Saints" in the Catholic Dictionary in Catholic Culture. Based on Fr. John Hardon's Modern Catholic Dictionary, © Eternal Life. Used with permission. https://www.catholicculture.org/culture/library/dictionary/index.cfm?id=36247&randomterm=false.

69 cf. Fr. Kevin in "Home at Last," edited by Rosalind Moss.

70 "UCI to shift anti-doping controls to new international body" in VeloNew. February 1, 2020.

  https://www.velonews.com/news/uci-to-shift-anti-doping-controls-to-new-international-body/.

71 Cardinal Cantalamessa, Raniero. Life in Christ. Collegeville, Minnesota: Liturgical Press. Kindle Edition. (pp. 5-6).

72 cf. Libreria Editrice Vaticana. Catechism of the Catholic Church (Kindle Location 1617). United States Conference of Catholic Bishops. Kindle Edition, nn. 774-775.

73 cf. Thomas Woods. How the Catholic Church Built Western Civilization. Washington DC: Regnery Publishing. 2005.

74 "Redemptoris Mater" (Mother of the Redeemer) by St. John Paul II. March 25, 1987, n. 45. Redemptoris Mater (25 March 1987) | John Paul II (vatican.va).

75 cf. Luke 1:39-56; Luke 2:15-20; Matthew 2:1-12; John 2:1-11.

76 "Do Catholics Have to Believe in Approved Apparitions?" Fr. Charles Grondin in Catholic Answers Q & A - https://www.catholic.com/qa/do-catholics-have-to-believe-in-approved-apparitions.

77 cf. "In Italy, cyclists bike to the church of their patron saint" in Aleteia, 6/5/21. https://aleteia.org/2021/06/05/cyclists-in-the-italian-alps-make-a-pilgrimage-to-this-church-dedicated-their-patron-saint/.

78 cf. Ibid.

79 cf. Ibid.

80 Ibid.

81 cf. Aili McConnon & Andres McConnon. Road to Valor: A True Story of World War II Italy, the Nazis, and the Cyclist Who Inspired a Nation. Publisher: Tantor Audio Release date: 06-12-12., 7-30.

82 cf. "Gino Bartali" in Wikipedia. https://en.wikipedia.org/wiki/Gino_Bartali.

83 cf. Aili McConnon & Andres McConnon. Road to Valor..., 41-42.

84 cf. Ibid.

85 cf. "Gino Bartali" in Wikipedia. https://en.wikipedia.org/wiki/Gino_Bartali.

86 cf. Aili McConnon & Andres McConnon. Road to Valor..., Chapter 6.

87 cf. Ibid., 101.

88 cf. Ibid., 111-115.

89 cf. Ibid., 243-245

90 cf. "Gino Bartali" in Wikipedia. https://en.wikipedia.org/wiki/Gino_Bartali.

91 cf. Ibid.

92 cf. "1946 Italian general election" in Wikipedia. https://en.wikipedia.org/wiki/1946_Italian_general_election.

93 cf. "Palmiro Togliatti" in Wikipedia. https://en.wikipedia.org/wiki/Palmiro_Togliatti.

94 cf. Aili McConnon & Andres McConnon. Road to Valor..., 204-209.

95 cf. "Gino Bartali" in Wikipedia. https://en.wikipedia.org/wiki/Gino_Bartali.

96 cf. Aili McConnon & Andres McConnon. Road to Valor..., 224-231.

97 cf. "Gino Bartali" in Wikipedia. https://en.wikipedia.org/wiki/Gino_Bartali.

98 cf. Ibid.

99 cf. "Gino Bartali" in Wikipedia. https://en.wikipedia.org/wiki/Gino_Bartali.

100 cf. Aili McConnon & Andres McConnon. Road to Valor..., 96.246-249.

101 cf. "Gino Bartali" in Wikipedia. https://en.wikipedia.org/wiki/Gino_Bartali.

102 cf. Ibid.

103 cf. Aili McConnon & Andres McConnon. Road to Valor..., 251-254.

104 cf. 'Gino Bartali' in Wikipedia. https://en.wikipedia.org/wiki/Gino_Bartali.

105 cf. Ibid.

106 cf. Aili McConnon & Andres McConnon. Road to Valor…, 35-36.

107 cf. "Gino Bartali" in Wikipedia. https://en.wikipedia.org/wiki/Gino_Bartali.

108 cf. Aili McConnon & Andres McConnon. Road to Valor…, 54-56.

109 Libreria Editrice Vaticana. Catechism of the Catholic Church (Kindle Location 1617). United States Conference of Catholic Bishops. Kindle Edition, "Rosary" in Glossary.

110 Cf. Ibid., n. 971.

111 Cf. "The Rosary," a tract in Catholic Answers. https://www.catholic.com/tract/the-rosary.

112 cf. Libreria Editrice Vaticana. Catechism of the Catholic Church (Kindle Location 1617). United States Conference of Catholic Bishops. Kindle Edition, n. 905.

113 cf. Ibid., n. 1350. 1357.1359.1365-1368.

Printed in Great Britain
by Amazon

54329927R00084